BABY TOUCH

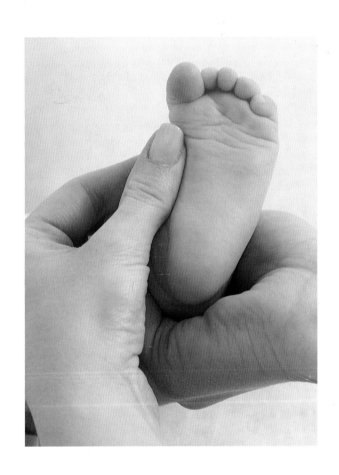

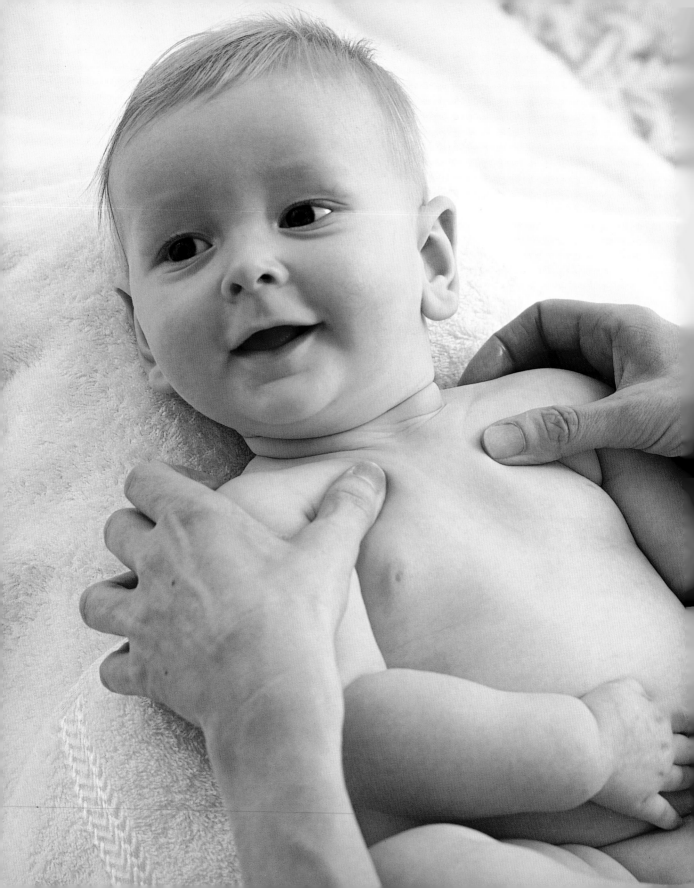

BABY TOUCH

WENDY KAVANAGH

SARAH SHEARS
CONSULTANT REFLEXOLOGIST

hamlyn

First published in Great Britain in 2005 by Hamlyn,
a division of Octopus Publishing Group Ltd
2–4 Heron Quays, London E14 4JP

Distributed in the United States and Canada by Sterling Publishing Co., Inc.
387 Park Avenue South, New York, NY 10016–8810

ISBN 0 600 61346 1
EAN 9780600613466

A CIP catalogue record for this book is available from the British Library

Printed and bound in China

10 9 8 7 6 5 4 3 2 1

Note: Massage and reflexology should not be considered
as replacements for professional medical treatment: a
physician should be consulted in all matters relating to
health and especially in relation to any symptoms which
may require diagnosis or medical attention. While the
advice and information in this book are believed to be
accurate, neither the author nor the publisher can accept
any legal responsibility for any injury sustained whilst
following any of the suggestions made herein.

CONTENTS

Infant massage, an ancient tradition in many cultures, is being rediscovered in the West. Around the world there are few places where babies are not massaged as a crucial but routine part of their care during the first few years of their life. Different cultures have different reasons for using massage. In Indonesia, for example, massage is used for babies with stomach pains whereas, in Russia, physicians teach mothers to massage newborn babies to enhance the development of their central nervous system. The benefit of baby touch is common to all.

INTRODUCTION

Intuitive baby massage has always been practised, but more formalized routines have only existed since the 1970s, after therapists visiting India experienced the positive effects of massage and combined it with elements of Swedish massage, reflexology and yoga stretches. Massaging babies and toddlers is now recognized as such an important tool that, in 1992, the School of Medicine at the University of Miami established the Touch Research Institute. The Director, Dr Tiffany Field, is renowned for her work and research programmes on infant massage and is dedicated to studying the effects of touch.

Like massage, reflexology has been practised for centuries as a form of natural healing. It is believed to have originated in China and is the forerunner of acupuncture. The Egyptians were also great believers in promoting healing and wellbeing through palpation of the feet. Pictorial evidence of a reflexology treatment being performed was discovered in the tomb of a physician, dated at about 2550 BC.

At the beginning of the twentieth century, an American ear, nose and throat specialist, Dr William Fitzgerald, rediscovered this ancient connection between pain relief and pressure points on the feet and hands. From this, he developed the technique known as 'zone therapy'. Eunice Ingham, the assistant of one of his colleagues, developed his technique further by mapping out the relationship of the body's structure and organs to the feet and hands. The 'Ingham method', as it is known, is the most closely related to reflexology as practised today. Growing in popularity, reflexology can be performed from birth, helping to develop the essential bond between parents and baby.

Massage and reflexology complement each other and are two of the most popular touch therapies. Dr Leboyer, a researcher in infant massage, believes that 'being touched and caressed, being massaged, is food for the infants'. New babies enjoy, need and crave touch, and baby touch is language at its best.

The application of touch through massage, and the benefits that it brings, has been well documented over the centuries. The message is clear: touch therapies are good for us and pave the way for a healthier, happier and calmer life. They provide both physiological and emotional benefits for babies and toddlers, as well as a means of soothing and comforting them that can be continued throughout their growing years. It is well documented that outcomes ranging from weight gain in pre-term infants to heightening awareness can be achieved through touch.

THE BENEFITS OF BABY TOUCH

PHYSIOLOGICAL BENEFITS

* Stimulates the circulation, thus increasing the flow of oxygen and nutrients around the body. This is important for newborn babies, whose extremities often seem cold until their circulatory system is fully developed.

* Stimulates the digestive tract, encouraging the passage of food and the elimination of waste, thus helping to relieve colic and constipation. In addition, stimulation of the main nerve to the digestive tract (the vagus) encourages the release of enzymes that digest the food, so that it can be absorbed, and hormones, such as glucagon and insulin, which together control blood sugar levels. Research has shown that premature babies who receive regular massage absorb food and gain weight faster than those who do not receive regular massage.

* Encourages the production of growth hormones from the pituitary gland.

* Stimulates the flow of lymph in the lymphatic system, the body's main line of defence against infection. This boosts the immune system, which is vital to the baby's resistance to infection.

* Encourages muscular coordination, helping babies to open out and straighten their limbs, thus improving joint flexibility.

* Stimulates the central nervous system, which is very important for both neurological and motor development.

* Improves the condition of the skin by helping cell regeneration and encouraging the release of sebum, the natural oil that improves elasticity and resilience.

* Aids recovery from specific childhood ailments, including asthma, catarrh, restless sleep, digestive complaints, skin problems, teething and earache.

EMOTIONAL BENEFITS

* Stimulates the release of endorphins, the 'happy' hormones that induce feelings of wellbeing and also act as pain-relievers.

* Stimulates sensory awareness by providing physical contact.

* Promotes reassurance, emotional security and trust.

* Reduces anxiety and trauma by reducing the production of cortisol, the stress hormone. This is very effective for babies who experienced a difficult birth, such as a caesarean delivery.

* Reinforces the bond between parent and child, which is very important in the formation of early relationships. It is a great way for a father to become more in touch with his baby, and for a mother with postnatal depression to overcome any negative feelings.

* Promotes calmness, relaxation and can sometimes be sleep-inducing, helping with teething and insomnia.

COMBINING MASSAGE AND REFLEXOLOGY

Reflexology is the perfect complement to a massage routine. This kind of touch focuses on specific problem areas around the body using simple techniques that you can integrate into your massage sequence. It combines the therapeutic and calming aspects of hands-on touch with the remedial effects of stimulating the reflex points on the feet.

The natural place in the massage routine to introduce any reflexology techniques that you feel are appropriate is following foot massage (see pages 60–61).

Like massage, reflexology can start from the day your baby is born and will have the same physiological and emotional benefits. The result will be a happy, healthy baby.

Choosing the right time to massage your baby makes all the difference to the enjoyment of the experience. By observing some basic rules, you, as the giver, will gain more confidence and this, in turn, will make your baby more relaxed. It is important only to massage your baby if she is in good health. If she seems lethargic or unwell, consult your doctor beforehand. It is important that both baby and parent are happy and relaxed so that the massage experience becomes an enjoyable one they can both look forward to.

DOS AND DON'TS

MASSAGE CHECKLISTS

Remember to observe the following rules.

Dos

* Do get your baby's permission before beginning a massage. Do this by observing her verbal or non-verbal signals.

* Do try again later in the day if your baby does not respond positively.

* Do be consistent with the timing of massage, building up a routine that your baby will eagerly anticipate.

* Do seek professional advice if your baby feels unwell. Massage is used to improve the body's own power of healing but it is not a substitute for medication.

* Do stop massaging and comfort your baby if she becomes distressed.

Don'ts

* Don't massage your baby if she has not had a full health assessment. This is usually carried out at 6–8 weeks of age. There are exceptions to this rule; for example, a tailored form of touch may be used to benefit premature or newborn babies.

* Don't massage if your baby is tired or hungry. An ideal time is 1–1½ hours after feeding.

* Don't massage your baby if she has been vaccinated within the previous week or is still suffering from the after-effects of vaccination.

* Don't massage your baby if she has a skin rash, infection or is being given any medication.

* Don't massage your baby if she has any joint problems, brittle bones or fractures.

* Don't massage your baby against her will or disturb her sleep in order to give a massage.

REFLEXOLOGY CHECKLISTS

There are some additional dos and don'ts for performing reflexology on your baby.

Dos

* Do keep the pressure light.

* Do trust your instincts.

* Do make sure that it is fun. Treat it as a game.

Don'ts

* Don't work on your baby's feet for more than 10 minutes but, at the same time, don't rush the sequence.

* Don't apply harsh pressure.

When you have gone through the checklists, don't forget to make sure that you, as the giver, are also relaxed and in good health.

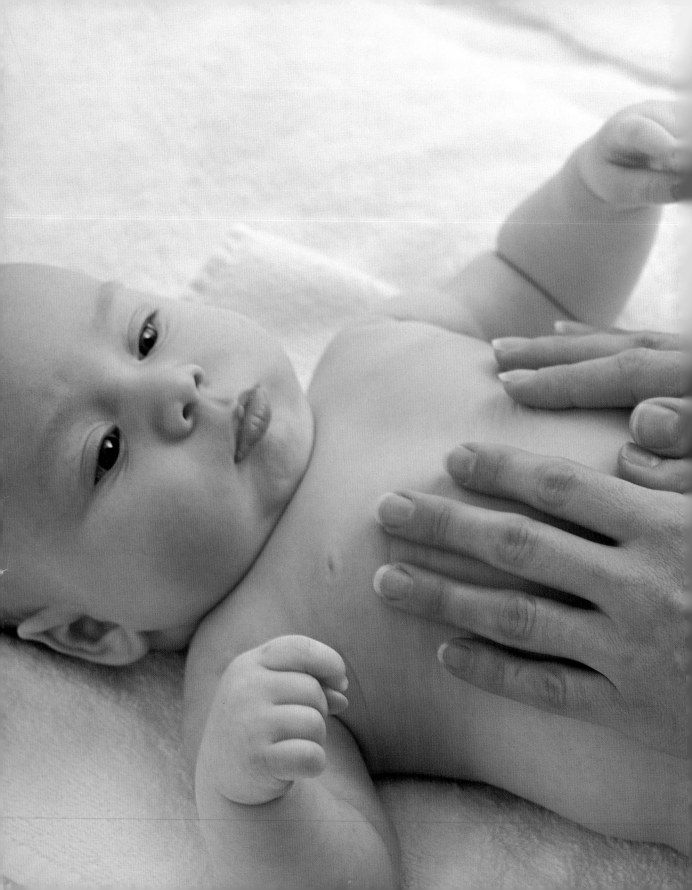

GETTING
STARTED

MASSAGE

Massaging babies or toddlers can be quite challenging because they often want to take an active part in the proceedings. Good preparation will create the relaxed environment that is central to the success of any touch therapy, making it a fun and pleasurable experience you will both want to repeat.

PREPARATION

THE ENVIRONMENT

Choose an area of your home where you enjoy spending time together and make this the regular place for massage. In this way, your baby or toddler will associate this area with touch. Clear a space so that you have room to move around, making sure that it is free from obstructions and dangerous objects or appliances. Remove anything that might fall on your child, such as hot drinks or candles.

Your chosen room should be warm and free from draughts because babies lose body heat much faster than adults. An even 26°C (80°F) is comfortable for massage. If there is no daylight, make sure that the lighting is soft and easy on the eye.

Peace and quiet with the minimum of distractions is essential, so make sure that the television, radio, telephone, or even the household pet, will not interrupt you. You may decide to play some soothing background music to enhance the atmosphere and set the scene.

THE GIVER

Wear comfortable, loose clothing and wash your hands, making sure that they are warm and clean. Remove any jewellery and your watch, and make sure that you have no rough skin, or long or jagged fingernails, that could harm your baby's delicate skin. Have some tissues or a kitchen roll to hand in case you need to remove any excess oil or lotion from your hands during the massage. You should be focused and relaxed in order to keep your massage rhythmic and flowing.

THE RECEIVER

Ideally, your baby should be unclothed for most full body massage routines. However, you may prefer to leave his nappy on to start with, until he feels less vulnerable and relaxes. Once your baby is naked, clean his skin, especially around the nappy area, and have plenty of warm soft towels at hand to keep him warm. It is also a good idea to have a nappy close to hand, together with some wipes, in case of any accidents.

As the giver, it is important to adopt positions that are comfortable and can be maintained for the length of the routine. Make sure your back is straight or supported to avoid any discomfort. As your baby grows, you will intuitively change and adapt these positions to suit you both.

POSITIONS

SITTING

Lay your baby on the floor, facing you, with a changing mat or towel beneath him for hygiene and comfort. If you sit with your legs stretched out on either side of your baby, you may need to support your back against a wall or a solid prop, such as a couch. Alternatively, sit on the edge of a cushion with your legs straddled or crossed. Another sitting position is to place your feet flat on the floor with your knees raised, using your thighs to support your baby.

Make sure that you can lean forward comfortably from any sitting position without putting a strain on your back.

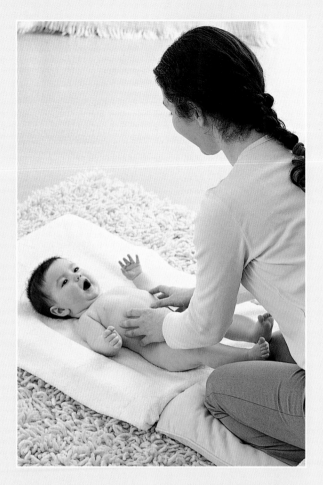

KNEELING

Place a pillow or towel under your knees and another between your bottom and your feet. Then sit back comfortably with your arms and shoulders in a relaxed position. For a full massage, you can either kneel at the foot of your baby or, with a small toddler, place him between your knees for support.

AIDED SUPPORT

By the time your baby is 2 or 3 months old, his neck and shoulders will be strong enough for him to hold up his head in line with his chest. Once he has reached this stage, you can sit him up to receive massage. In the kneeling position, place your baby in front of you, facing you, with his feet together and knees open. Then place one arm around his chest for support, leaving your other hand free to apply the massage.

UNAIDED SUPPORT

Once your baby is accustomed to sitting with
your help, he can progress to sitting unaided.
Babies are usually ready for this at about 7
months of age, when they can raise themselves
from a lying position and support themselves
on their hands and straightened arms. In the
kneeling position, place your baby between
your knees to improve his confidence and to
offer support if necessary. You can modify some
of the massage strokes, concentrating on those
that will be most beneficial in this position.

ORIENTAL STYLE

In the kneeling position, place your baby in front
of you between your knees, facing away from you
and kneeling with legs tucked underneath her.
Once your baby has reached the transitional
stage between sitting and crawling, this position
will be more natural. She will intuitively sit back
on her feet with her knees together. If you notice
that her feet turn outwards when in this position,
encourage them to turn inwards because this is
healthier for the development of the hips and
knees. It may be more of a challenge to massage
in this position as, once mobile, no baby wants
to stay still for too long.

If you apply massage directly to your baby's skin, you will need to use a lubricant (the massage medium) to enable your hands to glide across the skin without dragging and interrupting the flow of the stroke. This is especially important in baby touch because a baby's skin is so soft and delicate. There are many types of massage media available, some of which are specifically formulated for infants. It is very important to select a massage medium that is suitable for your baby and that you will find easy and comfortable to use.

MASSAGE MEDIA

A baby's skin is very sensitive and prone to allergies, so you should patch-test any massage medium before using it. Apply a small amount of your chosen medium over a little area of your baby's skin and, after 30 minutes, check to see whether there is any reaction. If a reaction occurs, try an alternative medium.

OILS

Any oils that you use should be non-greasy and pure. The skin easily absorbs natural oils so you may have to reapply the oil during the massage. Cold-pressed vegetable oils are the most effective, and they are rich in vitamins and minerals. Contrary to popular belief, clear baby oils are not suitable for massage because they are mineral oils and do not penetrate the skin. They are designed to retain moisture and act as a barrier on the skin's surface.

Almond oil is a light oil with excellent properties for dry and inflamed skin. Grapeseed oil is very gentle and is also one of the purest oils, which makes it easily absorbed. Coconut oil is popular in India for baby massage, and fractionated coconut oil has been used for premature babies because of its lack of allergens. Jojoba, sunflower and olive oils are all suitable, as well as being inexpensive and easily obtainable. There are a number of pre-blended massage oils formulated specifically for babies and toddlers, but these are not recommended for babies under 3 months old. They can be useful for specific ailments, but it is important to follow the instructions carefully.

CREAMS

Massage creams not only help the gliding movements but also nourish dry skin. A light-textured cream containing vitamin E is ideal. However, if you are already using a special cream to treat a skin condition, you can use this as your massage medium, combining daily treatments with massage.

GELS AND LOTIONS

These are both alternatives to oil. However, gels are oil-based and lotions are water-based, which means that you only need a small amount for massage. You must also be careful to remove any residue because these media are more slippery than oils and creams.

WAXES AND BALMS

Organic beeswax is a relatively new massage product that you can use in its pure form or as a professionally mixed essential oil combination to promote relaxation. Propolis, a natural substance that is found in bee balm, is often referred to as 'nature's antibiotic'. It is excellent for nourishing the skin and helps with nappy rash and similar skin conditions commonly occurring in babies.

TIP
Whichever medium you choose, keep it close to hand, in a spill-proof container, during the massage routine.

For babies, we use the 'mother' strokes of Swedish massage. These consist of effleurage (gliding), petrissage (squeezing), tapotement (percussion), friction and stretching. All these movements can be applied at different speeds and pressures, but the key to a good massage is to develop rhythm and flow and to maintain contact. In general, all massage is towards the heart, following the flow of blood in the veins, and pressure is applied on the upstroke and lifted on the return stroke. Before you start, warm your hands and give them a good shake to relax them.

BASIC MASSAGE
TECHNIQUES

EFFLEURAGE

This is the simplest technique to perform, and takes its name from the French word *effleurer*, meaning 'to touch lightly'. You apply this smooth, gliding stroke with the flat of your hand, keeping your fingers together. You can use both hands simultaneously on a larger baby but, on a very small baby, your fingers remain in contact rather than your whole hand. Use light pressure initially, increasing it as your baby grows and becomes more accustomed to receiving massage. A variation of this stroke is to cup your hands, which is useful when working on the arms and legs. For babies, you can use the flats of your hands in a backwards and forwards rubbing motion over the skin.

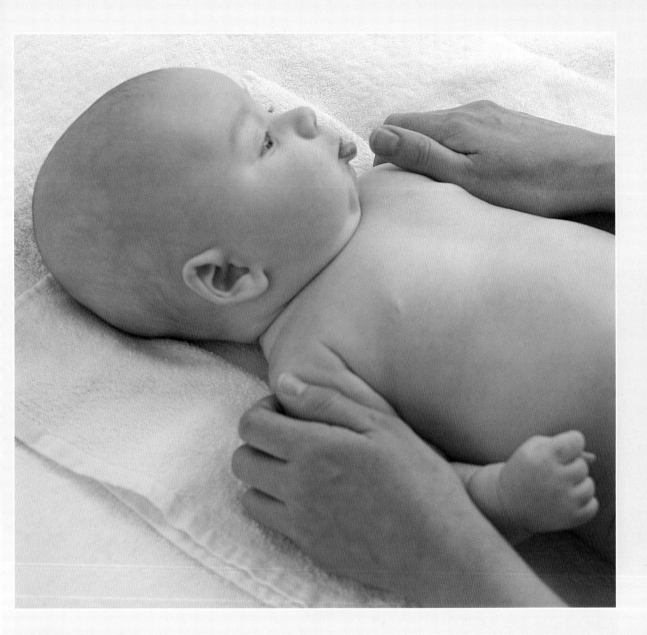

PETRISSAGE

This is the name given to any stroke that presses, squeezes and
rolls the tissue, and is derived from the French word *petrir*,
meaning 'to knead'. You can apply these strokes with one or both
hands and, in smaller areas, with the thumbs and fingers. Do not
use them on the fleshier areas of your baby's body, unless, or until,
the tissue is sufficiently dense.

TAPOTEMENT

This consists of a series of percussion strokes, so-called because of the noise they make, and includes hacking, cupping and flicking. The word 'tapotement' comes from the French word *tapoter*, meaning 'to tap'. You apply these strokes briskly in a rhythmic motion so you will not need any oil or cream. The sides of the fingers, cupped hands and thumbs and fingertips are all used to perform tapotement.

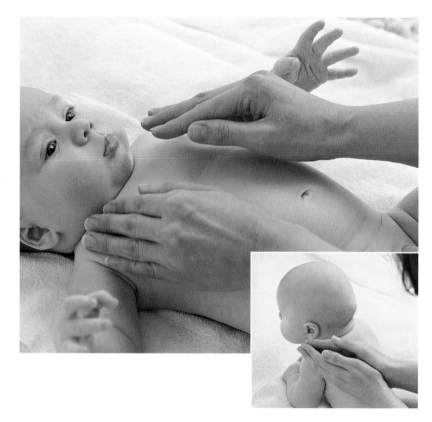

FRICTION

These are very focused movements that you apply with the pads of your fingers or thumbs or the heel of your hand. They are often made with one hand and little or no glide, so there is no need to apply oil or cream. In baby massage, apply light pressure, usually in a circular motion, as opposed to the deeper stroke used for adults.

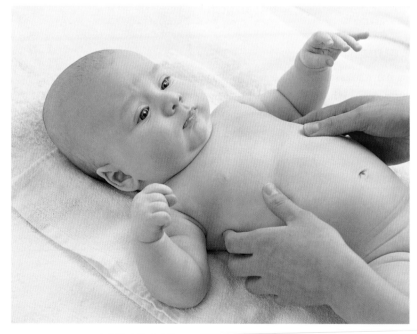

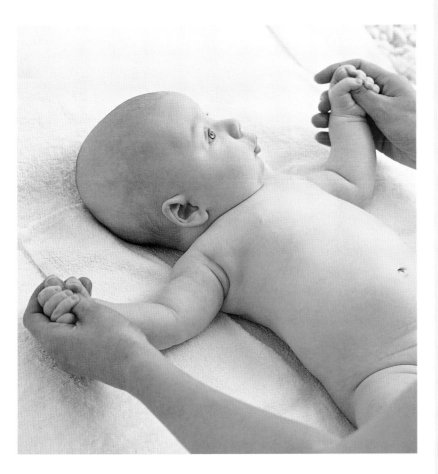

MASSAGE STROKES

Each massage stroke has its own properties. Effleurage is a relaxing, soothing stroke that introduces the massage and helps to apply the massage medium. It also increases circulation. Petrissage and friction release tension from the muscles and increase nutrient flow and the elimination of waste, while stretching increases joint mobility and flexibility and adds fun and variety to the massage.

STRETCHING

In baby massage, it is very important that any gentle stretching is only done when the baby is fully relaxed and so tends to be performed at the end of a massage session. If your baby has any joint problems do not attempt any stretching techniques.

REFLEXOLOGY

The aim of reflexology is to identify and release any blockages in the flow of energy through the body, thus increasing the body's natural ability to heal itself. As well as encouraging energy flow and the release of toxins, reflexology has a profound sedative effect on the whole body, encouraging relaxation and a sense of wellbeing.

HOW REFLEXOLOGY WORKS

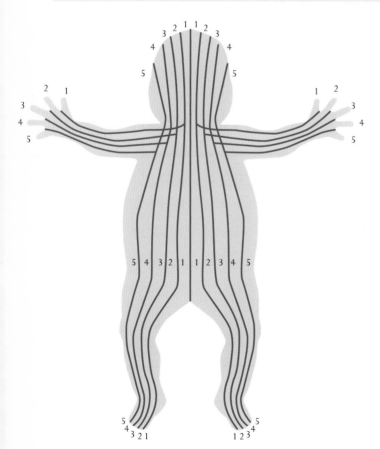

ZONES

Reflexology is based on the division of the body into ten energy zones which run the length of the body, from head to toe and down through the arms to the hands. *Qi* energy, (pronounced 'chee'), flows through these zones when we are in good health.

REFLEX POINTS

The systems and organs of the body are represented by reflex points on the feet (see pages 26–29), and these can help us to identify areas of the body where the energy is not properly balanced. By using a caterpillar-style or gliding stroke of your thumb or finger, and by applying light pressure over the reflex points, it is possible to detect energy blockages. These present themselves in the form of discomfort and crystalline deposits. Working generally over the reflex point will effectively treat the smaller reflex points undetectable on tiny feet.

BENEFITS

Stimulation of the reflex points
has a significant effect on
the nervous system, promoting
relaxation and helping to restore
its balance. Reflex stimulation
of the nervous system triggers a
calming influence on the internal
organs and muscle function.

REFLEXOLOGY MEDIA

Most reflexologists use powder to ease the movement of the fingers and thumbs over the foot, and this is ideal if you are applying reflexology alone. However, if you are incorporating reflexology into a massage routine, you can continue to use a fine oil, but in minimal amounts. If your baby has a skin complaint, such as eczema or psoriasis, you may choose to use a light moisturizing cream. Whichever medium you find it appropriate to use, remember that it should only be used in small amounts. Excess use will make the reflexology experience messy and less enjoyable for both mother and baby.

TIP

The beauty of reflexology is that it
is easy to learn, quick to apply,
doesn't require the removal of
clothing other than socks, and can be
performed absolutely anywhere.

25

The following pictorial gallery is designed to clearly identify the main reflex points used to treat minor baby ailments. Once you have mastered the basic techniques for a simple reflexology routine, shown on pages 30–35, you can incorporate these reflex points for maximum effectiveness. Include all of the points if you wish to perform a reflexology treatment for the whole of the body, or choose specific points to treat particular ailments as discussed in Treating Common Ailments on pages 82–109.

REFLEX POINTS

ZONES

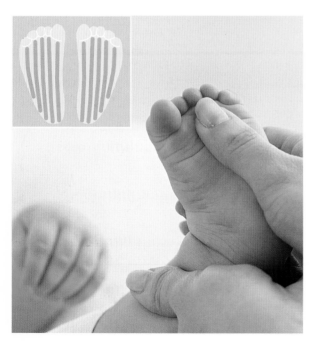

SPINE

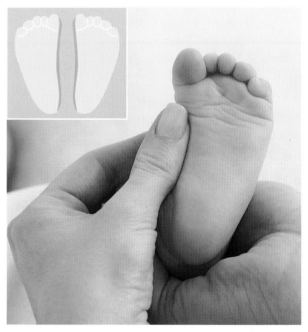

HEAD

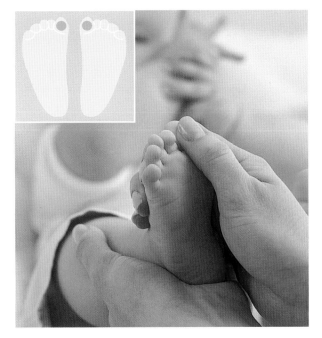

SINUSES

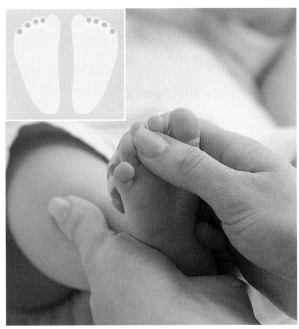

TEETH

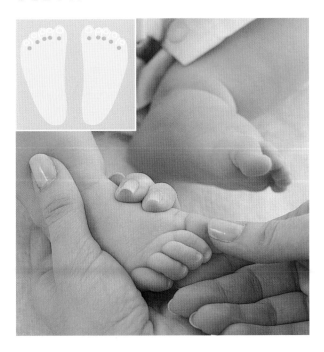

EARS

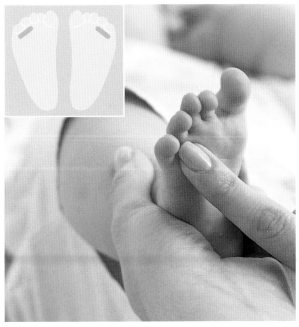

EUSTACHIAN TUBE

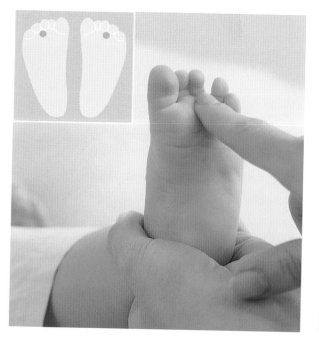

LYMPHATICS

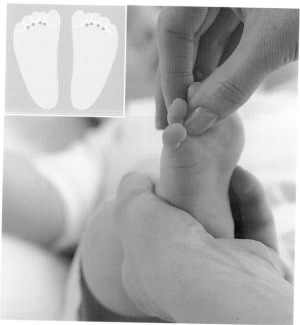

TRACHEA

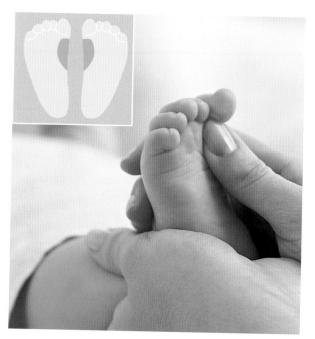

LUNGS

SOLAR PLEXUS

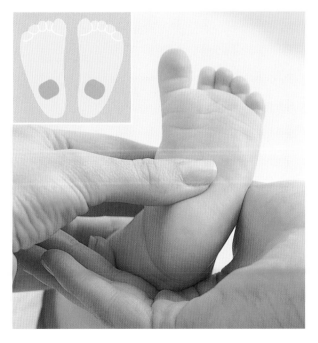

STOMACH

SMALL INTESTINE

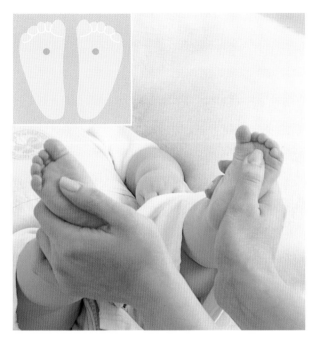

COLON

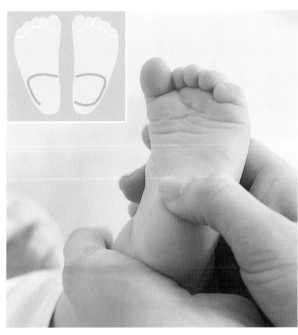

Start by learning these eight simple techniques. Your baby should not find any of the following techniques uncomfortable unless he is suffering from a common babyhood ailment. If so, he will instinctively respond by pulling away. However, babies often withdraw their feet in response to touch, so this reaction may not indicate true discomfort. Watching your baby's facial expressions will help you to monitor his discomfort levels.

BASIC·REFLEXOLOGY TECHNIQUES

CONNECTING ENERGY

To initiate contact, place the palms of your hands on the soles of your baby's feet so that he can connect with your energy. He will instinctively press his feet against you.

Once you and your baby have become familiar with each technique, you can begin to practice them in the sequence they are shown in here. After connecting energy with your baby and performing the solar plexus and cradling techniques on both his feet at once, practice each technique first on the right foot, then on the left.

SOLAR PLEXUS PRESS

Place both thumbs simultaneously on the solar plexus reflex points and allow your baby to press gently against you.

CRADLING TECHNIQUE

Support your baby's feet at the heels with the palms of your hands. Hold them loosely so that he can withdraw his feet if he wishes to do so.

ZONE-WALKING

With your baby's foot gently cradled in your hand, walk the thumb of your free hand in a caterpillar walk/zigzag-style movement through each zone from his heel to each toe along each energy zone of the foot (see boxed text, 'Caterpillar Walk'). Start at zone 1 of the heel. This movement will encourage energy flow.

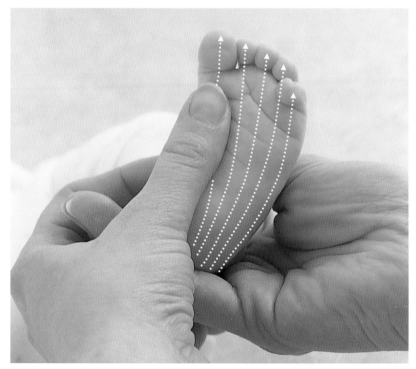

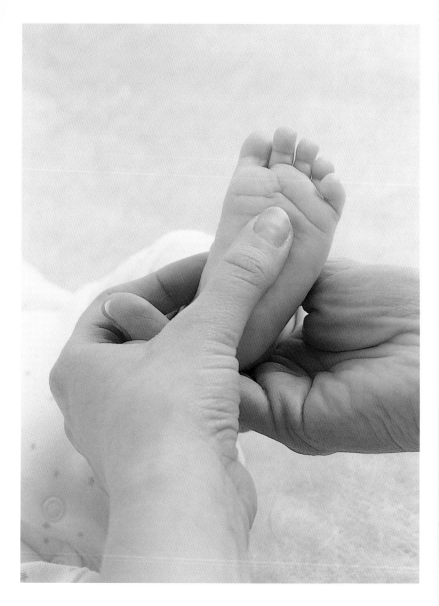

CATERPILLAR WALK

*Place your straight thumb on
the foot and gently alternately
bend and straighten the thumb
at the joint as you move your
thumb across or up the foot.
This bending and straightening
movement gives the appearance
of a caterpillar walking.*
Note: *This movement can be
performed with the thumb or finger
but is described here with the thumb.*

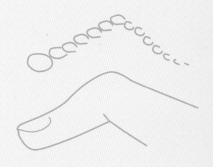

GLIDING TECHNIQUE

At first, you may find the caterpillar-walk strange, or your baby
may not allow you time to do it. As an alternative you can glide
your thumb through each zone in the same way. You may also
choose to use this in addition to zone-walking in order to
enhance the treatment.

SPINAL WALK

Apply either the caterpillar walk or a gliding stroke from your baby's inner heel up through the spinal reflex point and over the top of his big toe. This will help to relax his nervous system.

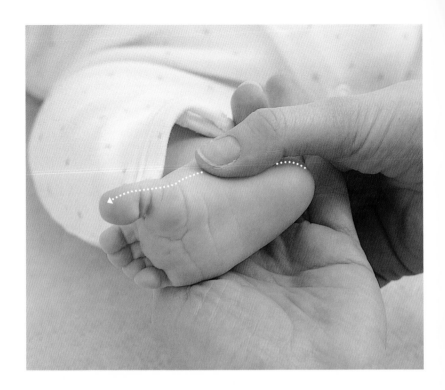

PRESSURE TECHNIQUE

With your baby's foot still loosely cradled in your hand, gently press the centre of the pad of each toe in turn with the thumb of your free hand. Use your index finger to lightly support the toe being worked from behind.

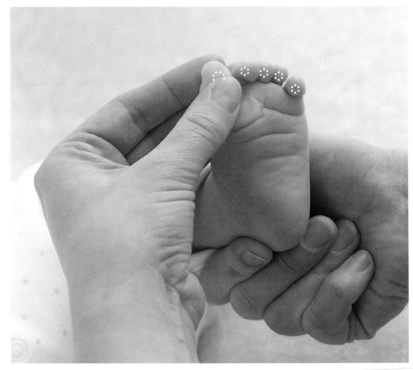

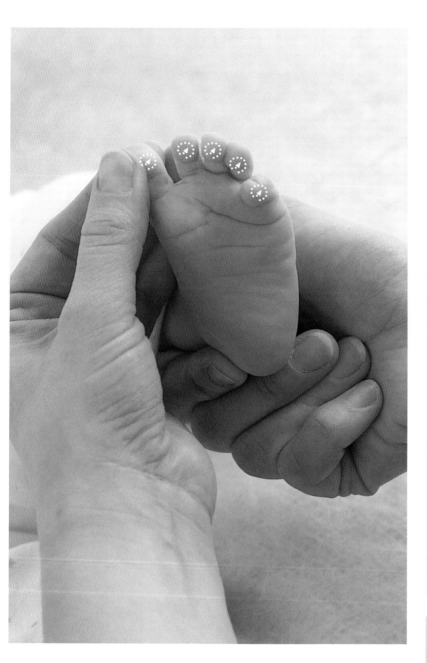

*These few techniques will equip
you with the skills to alleviate
a number of babyhood ailments.
Once you have established this
basic reflexology routine, you can
introduce ailment-related reflex
points (see Treating Common
Ailments, pages 82–109).
The caterpillar-walk, gliding
stroke, pressure and circling
techniques are all used on reflex
points related to specific ailments.*

CIRCLING PRESSURE TECHNIQUE

As in the pressure technique, press gently on the pad of each toe and then circle the pad of your thumb over the area. Continue to support your baby's toes from behind with your index finger.

TIP

*A few minutes of reflexology
is enough to be effective, so
don't be discouraged if your
baby only allows you to do
the basics at the start.*

AROUND-THE-BODY MASSAGE

If you have little or no experience of baby massage, it is essential to start gradually in order to familiarize yourself with the techniques, how much pressure to use and your baby's reaction. Start with a massage of 5–10 minutes and then, once you feel comfortable with this, incorporate additional strokes, gradually becoming more adventurous as your baby responds to your confidence. It may take three or four sessions for you and your baby to begin to enjoy the experience so don't give up: the end result is worth the perseverance.

DEVELOPING A ROUTINE

As your baby grows and develops, you can build on the 10-minute routine by introducing additional techniques and adopting different positions. Once he is about 2 months old, you can begin to practise a full massage routine, introducing a stage at a time until you and your baby are comfortable with a full massage session. You would normally start the sequence on the front of your baby's body, first working up the body and then from top to toe, so that your baby gets used to the routine. The same applies to the back. However, you may wish to massage specific areas, or add some reflexology if you feel it is appropriate. Some babies prefer a more gradual approach to massage, so start with their feet and legs, slowly working upwards. Remember that the effleurage stroke is the 'mother' stroke for massage; use it to spread the massage medium and to warm up an area before applying deeper strokes. It is also useful for connecting each part of your routine and to complete the massage.

AGE GUIDELINES
The following are some simple guidelines for massaging babies of different ages.

0–3 months
Although you would not normally give a full body massage until after your baby's post-natal check, you can use very light strokes on his head and back. Use the pads of your fingers rather than your whole hand to apply effleurage strokes on his hands and feet. You may wish to introduce specific techniques to relieve babyhood ailments such as colic, wind and constipation.

3–6 months
You can start to use a greater variety of strokes and apply some pressure as, by now, your baby will be more developed and his muscle tissue will be denser. The 10-minute routine (see pages 40–45) plus some stretching would be appropriate, and your baby may even feel

comfortable being massaged in a supported sitting position. Massage to relieve teething symptoms can be introduced at this stage.

6–9 months

Deeper strokes, such as friction and petrissage, can be applied with more pressure as your baby's limbs grow and his muscles develop. The massage sessions can be longer, but they may become more of a challenge as his mobility and curiosity increase. It may be helpful to set aside time shortly before your baby goes to bed, as he will be less active and more responsive.

9–12 months

At this stage, massage becomes even more of a challenge so you need to make it more of a game, with a less structured routine.

12–15 months

If you massage your baby regularly, he will look forward to his session so it is important to set aside a specific time for it. Your baby will start to give you signs of which strokes he likes and dislikes, and his mobility will continue to challenge the way that you massage.

15–18 months

By now, your toddler will have learned to accept baby touch as part of everyday life, and he may even be trying to copy some of your strokes. His increasing independence may mean shortening the massage time. Try new methods, such as head massage, while he is seated or having his hair washed. At this age, toddlers respond well to hand and foot massage while sitting on their mother's lap or being cuddled.

18 months onwards

There is no age limit to receiving massage. The main rule is to 'listen' to your child's needs and respect his touch boundaries. Massage should remain an enjoyable and positive experience for your child.

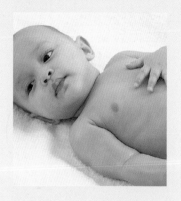

Once you and your baby are in a comfortable position, pour a little warm oil on to your hands. With the flat-handed effleurage stroke, start at the middle of his chest and glide up to his shoulders and down his arms, using enough pressure to avoid tickling. Repeat this until his skin has a sheen, taking care not to over-oil the skin. You are now ready to start your 10-minute routine.

10-MINUTE ROUTINE

CHEST AND ARMS

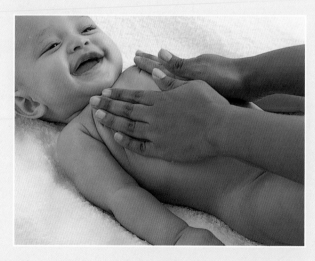

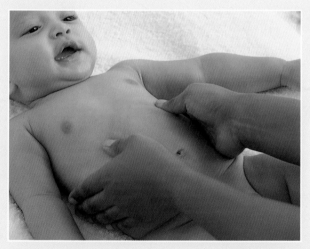

1 Place both hands, palms down, on either side of your baby's breastbone and gently push outwards to the edges of his ribcage on either side. Return to the centre of his chest, reducing the pressure but remaining in contact. Repeat this 3–4 times.

2 Place your hands at the base of your baby's breastbone and, using the pads of your thumbs in a friction stroke, work over his whole chest in tiny circular movements. Finish off by gliding both hands up his breastbone and along either side of his collarbone, ending with a stroke down his arms.

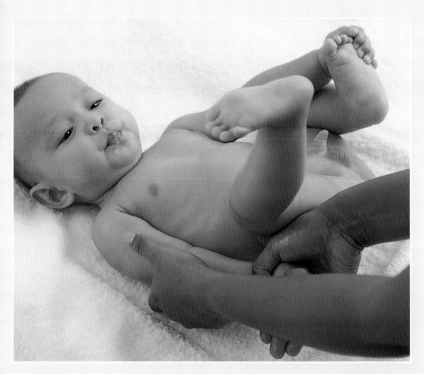

3 Work on one arm at a time, supporting your baby's lower arm with one hand. With the other hand, hold his upper arm between your thumb and fingers. With the pad of your thumb, make firm circles, working the whole area between his elbow and armpit. Finish with a gliding stroke over his chest and down his arm, as before.

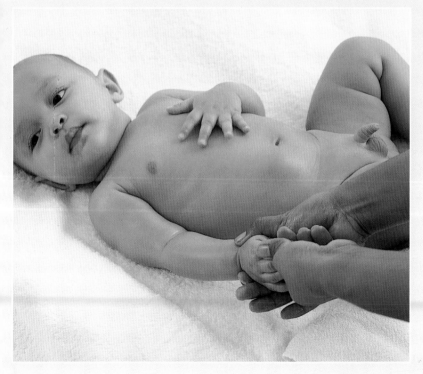

4 Move to your baby's lower arm and hand, and repeat the thumb-circling over the whole area. Use your index finger and thumb to massage his fingers. Repeat the whole sequence on his other arm and hand.

TIP

As a guideline, apply the same pressure when massaging your baby as you would do when wiping his nappy area.

ABDOMEN AND LEGS

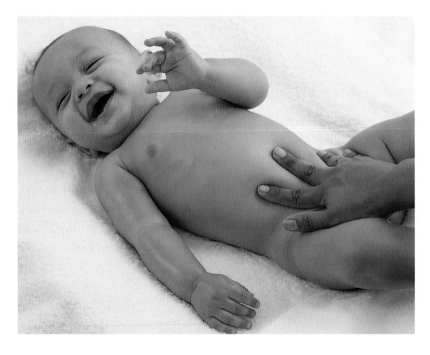

1 Place the heel of one hand just above your baby's genital region on the pubic bone. With open fingers, make a gentle sweeping stroke, working fan-like from his right side to his left side. Repeat this 3–4 times.

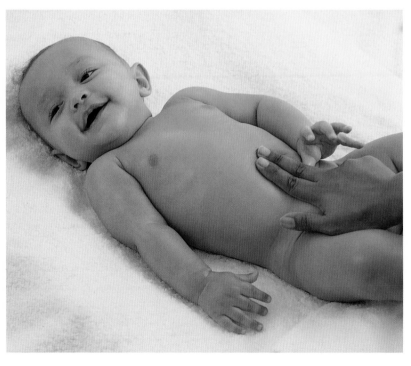

2 Starting at the bottom right of your baby's abdomen, and using the pads of your first two fingers, make gentle circular movements across the abdomen to the bottom left. Continue in ever-decreasing arcs until you have covered the whole area, finishing just above the genital area. Finish with a fanning motion and effleurage across his abdomen, chest and arms.

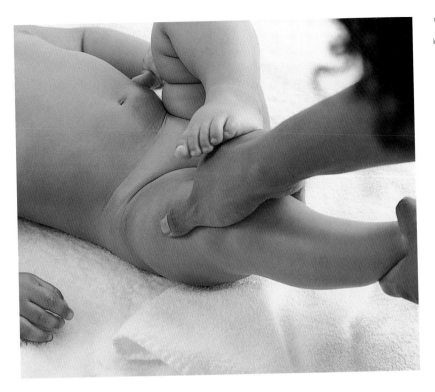

3 Support one leg under the ankle with one hand and, with the other hand, glide up and down his leg, applying the oil. Hold your baby's upper leg between your thumb and fingers and, with the pad of your thumb, make firm circles, working the whole area between his knee, hip and groin. Move to his lower leg and repeat the thumb-circling between the ankle and the knee. Finish by drawing little half moons on his knee. Repeat this on the other leg.

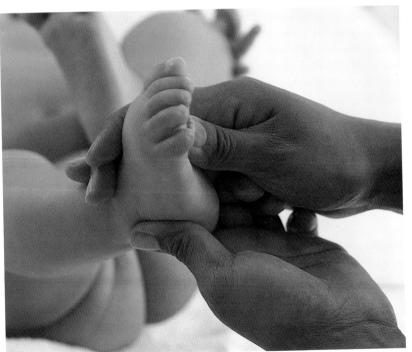

4 Supporting your baby's ankle with one hand use the index finger and thumb of your other hand to massage his foot. Finish with a gliding stroke down his sides, legs and feet. Repeat the sequence on his other leg and foot.

TIP

The abdomen is a sensitive area so you may need to reapply the oil because your massage needs to flow. Take care not to lean into the area during the massage.

BACK

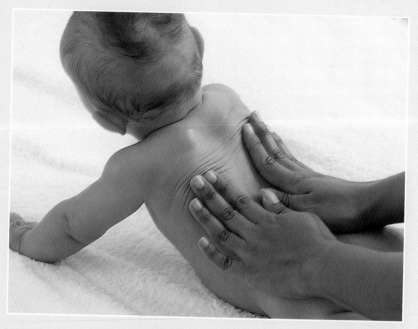

1 Using the gliding effleurage stroke, apply oil to your baby's buttocks and back. Then, using the pads of your thumb or fingers, work over the whole of his buttock area in small circles, up towards the back. Repeat this 3–4 times.

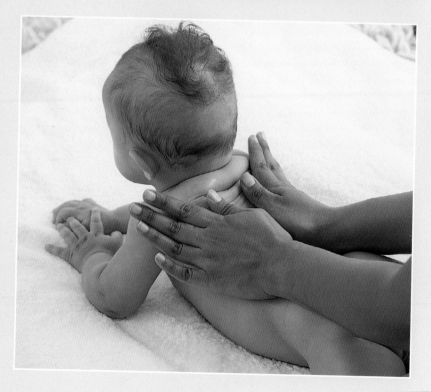

2 Using both hands, perform effleurage along either side of your baby's spine, along the tops of his shoulders and down the arms to his hands and fingers. Repeat this 3–4 times.

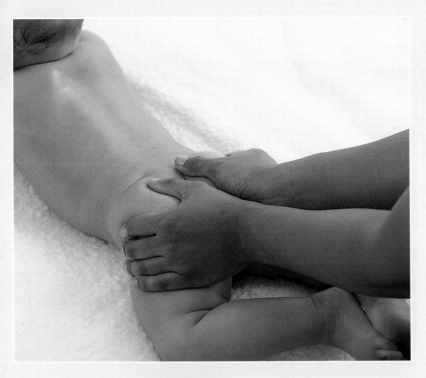

3 Starting at the base of your baby's spine, work with the pads of your thumbs or fingers in small circles, taking care not to apply pressure on the spine or neck area. Continue over the entire back and buttock area.

4 Finish with some gentle stroking from head to toe before wrapping your baby in a warm towel and giving him a loving cuddle.

TIP

Small babies may feel insecure when lying prone so you may need to work in stages, picking up your baby occasionally to reassure him. Don't rush things and you will end up with a routine that you both enjoy.

Once you are familiar with the basics of a full body massage, you can either work through the whole routine or tailor it to suit you and your baby. Vary the routine as your baby develops, adding interest to your massage. The sequence can be as long or as short as your baby's attention span allows and you can modify it to fit the time you have available. Massage is a very flexible form of touch.

FULL MASSAGE ROUTINE

CHEST

Specific massage routines for babyhood conditions relating to the chest are given later in the book (see pages 84–91). Meanwhile, regular massage will encourage your baby to open up her chest and develop a relaxed breathing pattern.

1 Sit in a comfortable position, with your baby facing you. Place the flats of your oiled hands on the centre of her chest and hold this position. Apply slight pressure and then slowly release it while still maintaining contact. Making the first touch in this way will reassure and relax your baby, preparing her for the following strokes.

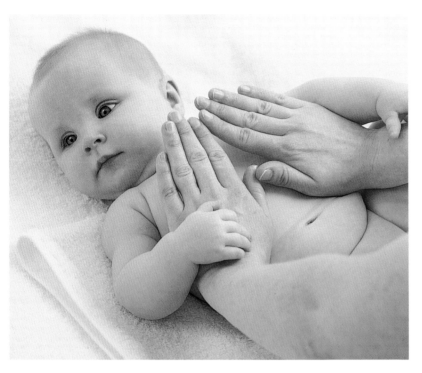

2 Keeping your thumbs in the centre of your baby's chest, use the heels of both hands to massage outwards and downwards around her lower rib cage and return. Repeat this 3–4 times.

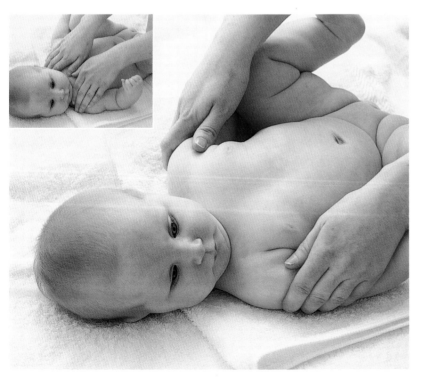

3 From the central position, and using the flat-handed effleurage stroke, massage upwards and outwards across your baby's shoulders and the tops of her arms, returning to the centre in one rhythmic sweep. Repeat this 3–4 times.

4 With your hands cupped slightly, use a percussion stroke to work lightly across the top and sides of your baby's chest. Continue this for 15 seconds.

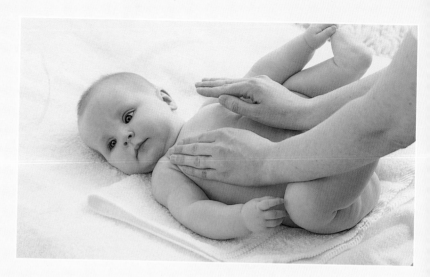

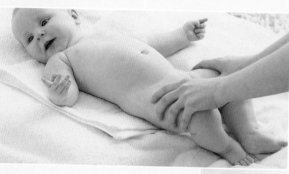

5 Using both hands from the central position, effleurage upwards and outwards across your baby's shoulders and the tops of her arms again. Return to the centre and continue down her trunk to her legs and feet. Without breaking contact, continue to work back up her body in reverse and finish by stroking down each arm. This should be one long sweeping stroke. Repeat this 3–4 times.

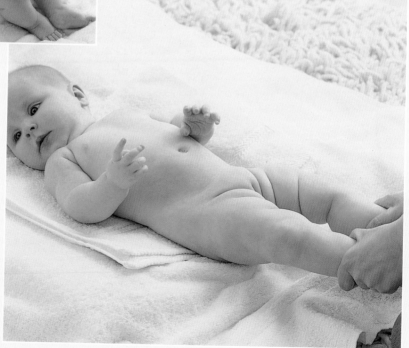

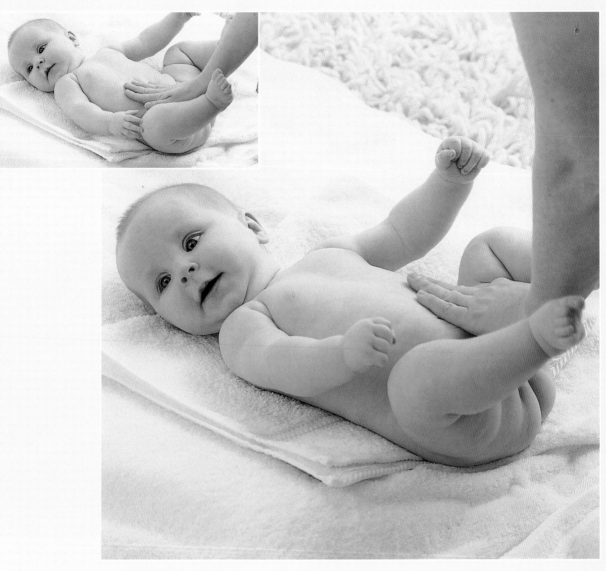

6 Using the fingers of one hand, stroke diagonally from the top of your baby's shoulder to the opposite hip. As you reach the end of your stroke, lift your other hand ready to repeat the movement on the other side. Imagine you are drawing an invisible X across the front of the chest, using your hands alternately. Repeat this 3–4 times.

TIP
Opening up the chest and rib cage area with this massage will improve breathing and reduce any build-up of tension resulting from crying.

ARMS

It takes some time for young babies to consciously open their arms because this requires both strength and coordination. Massage encourages babies to open their arms outwards until the movement becomes a natural reflex. Developing flexibility is very important for posture and also to encourage suppleness of the muscles.

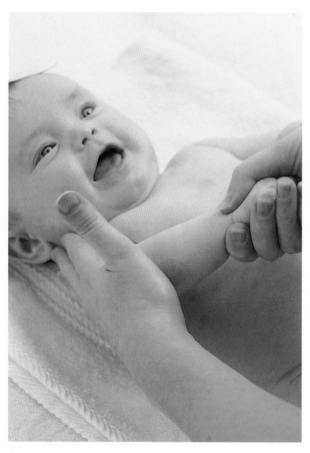

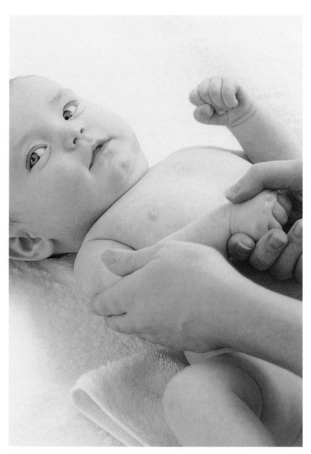

1 Take one of your baby's arms and, holding her wrist in one hand, glide your other hand in an effleurage stroke along her arm from the wrist to the top of the arm. Then turn your hand slightly outwards and return down the side of her arm with a gentle stretch. Repeat this 3–4 times.

2 Using a petrissage stroke, knead your baby's arm between your fingers and the heel of your hand, working along the length of the arm from the wrist to the top of the arm. Repeat steps 1 and 2 on the other arm.

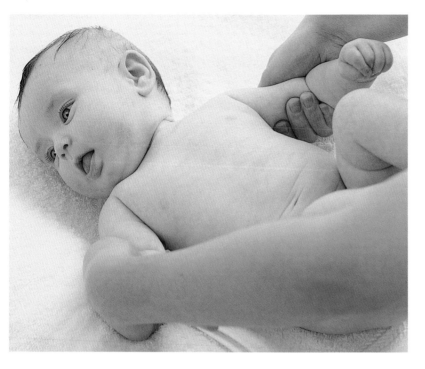

3 Working on both arms simultaneously, gently squeeze and release the muscles from the top of your baby's shoulders down to her hands between your fingers and thumbs.

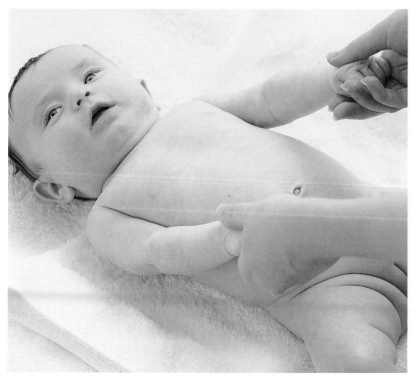

4 Starting at the top of her shoulders, take your baby's arms in the palms of your hands and gently pull the length of the arms through them, pulling downwards in line with the body. Gently squeeze your hands as you pull off. Repeat this 3–4 times.

TIP

In a young baby, it is a natural reflex to keep the arms close to the body. This sequence helps your baby to develop flexibility and coordination.

HANDS

Massaging the hands, the ultimate tool of touch, is probably one of the most instinctive forms of massage and it is so versatile that you can perform it anywhere or even make it part of play time. From the time when newborn babies grasp our fingers to the moment when they are able to hold objects, a period of up to 12 months, their hands are developing in strength and coordination. This communication through touch, like holding and caressing, is an important part of the bonding process.

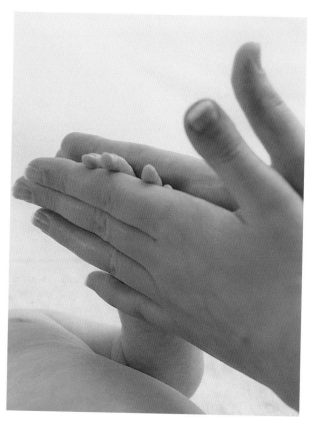

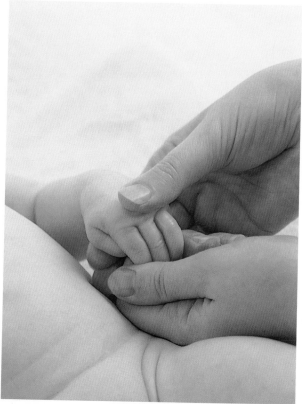

1 Take one of your baby's hands between the palms of your hands and rub it backwards and forwards in order to relax and straighten it. Continue this for 15 seconds.

2 With your fingers beneath your baby's hand and your thumbs on top, gently roll your thumbs backwards and forwards in very small movements, gradually working the whole area from the wrist to the base of the fingers.

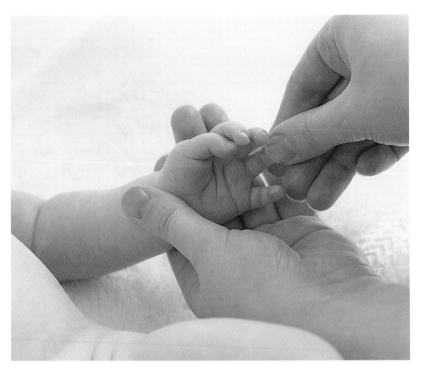

3 Take one finger between your index finger and your thumb and gently pull the length of the finger through your fingers, giving a gentle squeeze to the tip as you pull off. Repeat this on each finger.

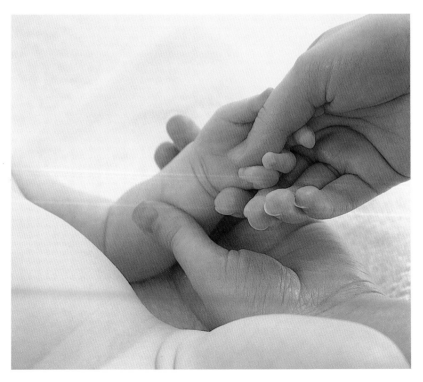

4 Turn the hand over and, with the pad of your thumb, make small circular movements over the palm, applying enough pressure to stretch your baby's hand open as you massage.

Repeat steps 1–4 on the other hand.

ABDOMEN

When massaging the abdomen, make sure that the umbilical cord area has healed. Your baby needs to be relaxed in order to enjoy massage over this very sensitive and emotional area so do not continue if she shows signs of anxiety. If she becomes upset, move on or pick her up and give her a cuddle before continuing. The area will feel taut if your baby is anxious but soft when she is relaxed. Take care not to apply too much pressure over the abdomen area as this may cause some discomfort to the underlying intestines and bladder.

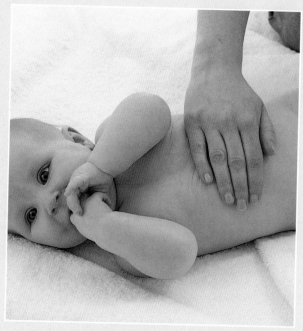

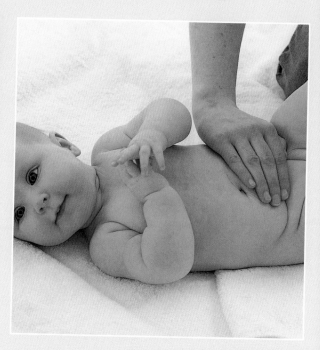

1 Make contact by placing the flat of your oiled hand over your baby's abdomen and holding it there for a moment. Hold her ankles with your other hand to support her legs. With the effleurage stroke, massage clockwise in a circular motion. Always work clockwise on this area, following the flow through the intestinal tract. Repeat this 3–4 times.

2 Next, cup your massaging hand and turn it to work horizontally across the area. Massage the area between her hips and lower ribs, working gently from side to side. Continue this for 15 seconds.

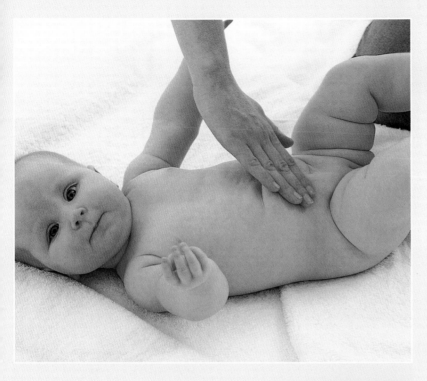

3 Staying in the same area, and with the pads of your fingers, use both hands alternately to massage your baby's left side between her hip and lower rib, drawing your hands across the area below the navel. Repeat this 3–4 times. Then move to your baby's right side and repeat the sequence.

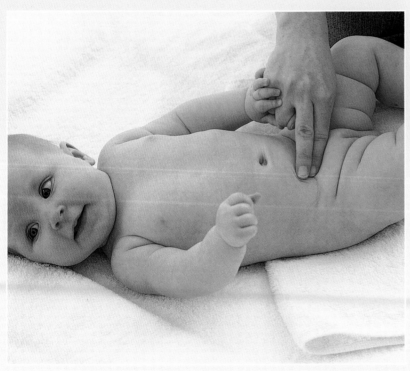

4 Move back to the centre of your baby's abdomen and repeat step 1, this time increasing the size of the circles to encompass the pubic bone and the area below the navel. Use the flat of the hand, or just the first and second fingers to focus the massage stroke. At this point, your baby may urinate or empty her bowel, so be prepared and have a towel or wipe to hand. This is a natural reaction because you are working over the area of the body where the bladder and colon are situated.

HIPS

The development of the hips plays a very important role in mobility and good posture. In early life, babies are extremely flexible, and regular massage will help maintain this flexibility as their body develops. End this massage sequence by gently shaking out your baby's legs and lightly stroking the whole of each leg from hip to toe.

1 With your baby facing you, hold her ankles with both of your hands and make sure her legs are relaxed. If not, try some very gentle shaking movements or playful positions to loosen them. Bend and straighten each of your baby's legs alternately, in a pedalling-like motion. Keep the movement smooth and flowing. Continue this for 15 seconds.

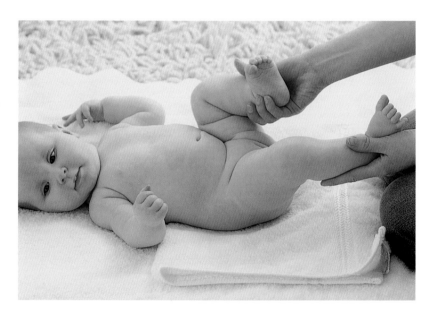

2 Press the flat of each foot together, toe to toe and heel to heel, and then release, making sure that your baby's knees bend outwards at all times. Do not force the positions and move on if your baby finds this uncomfortable. Otherwise continue this for 15 seconds.

3 With her knee still bent outwards, take your baby's right foot in your left hand, and place it down gently to rest on her navel. With your other hand, petrissage or rub her exposed buttock and the back of her thigh for about 20 seconds. Release her leg and gently straighten it. Repeat this on her other leg.

4 Repeat steps 1 and 2 and, while her feet are together, hold both her legs at the ankles with your right hand and place them gently down to rest on her navel. Hold this position and, with the flat of your left hand, massage around the base of her spine and buttock area. Continue this for 15 seconds.

TIP

Massaging the hips is especially beneficial for babies who like to stand before they can sit unaided and helps to avoid joint inflexibility.

LEGS

Massaging the legs promotes coordination and lower back strength. Up to the age of 3 months babies move their legs a great deal, building up their strength. This strength needs to be maintained for when they start to sit and stand. Massage will also promote flexibility in the joints of the knees and ankles as your baby develops.

1 Take your baby's right leg by holding her ankle in your right hand. With your oiled left hand, use the effleurage stroke to glide up her leg from ankle to hip and return down the side of her leg, applying pressure on the upward stroke. Repeat this 3–4 times.

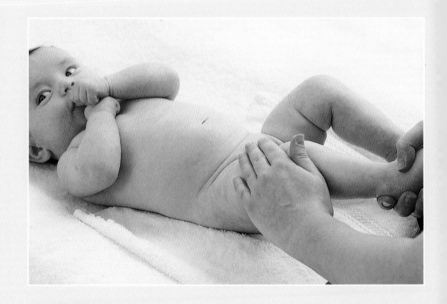

2 With your fingers under your baby's thigh and your thumb on top, use the pad of your thumb to make small circular movements, massaging the whole of the thigh. Repeat steps 1 and 2.

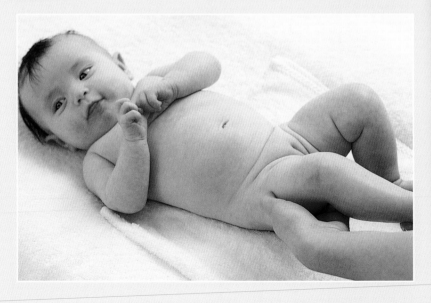

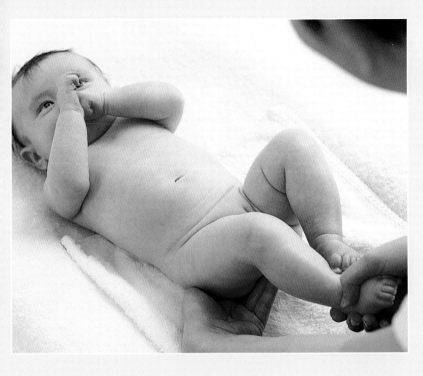

3 In a petrissage stroke, gently squeeze your baby's leg between the heel of your hand and your fingers, working from the top of her thighs to her ankles. Repeat steps 1–3 on the other leg.

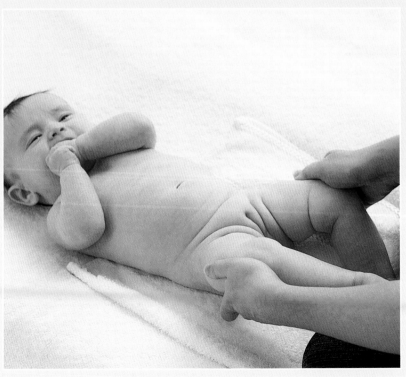

4 Rest your hands on your baby's inner thighs and then glide outwards and down the back of her legs to her ankles with a gentle pressure, enough to straighten her legs. Return up the front of her legs to her thighs. Repeat this 3–4 times.

TIP
Leg massage helps your baby to develop the ability to sit, stand and walk.

FEET

Massaging the feet can be very relaxing as long as your touch is firm and your focus is on the tops and sides of the feet, which are less sensitive or ticklish than the undersides. Foot massage helps the feet to open out, preparing them for the time when your baby starts to stand.

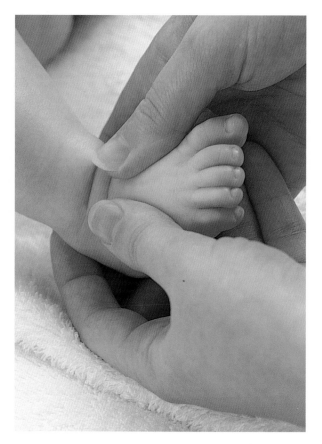

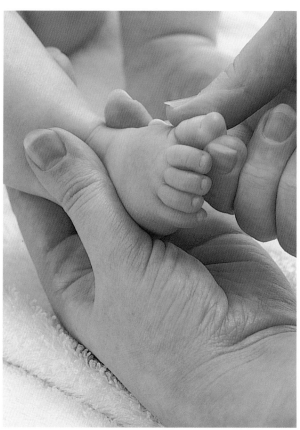

1 Take your baby's foot in both hands, with the sole resting on your fingers and your thumbs on the top of her foot, and glide the pads of your thumbs backwards and forwards over the whole area. Continue this for 15 seconds.

2 Take each toe, one by one, between the pads of your index finger and thumb and gently roll it backwards and forwards, separating each toe as you work along her foot.

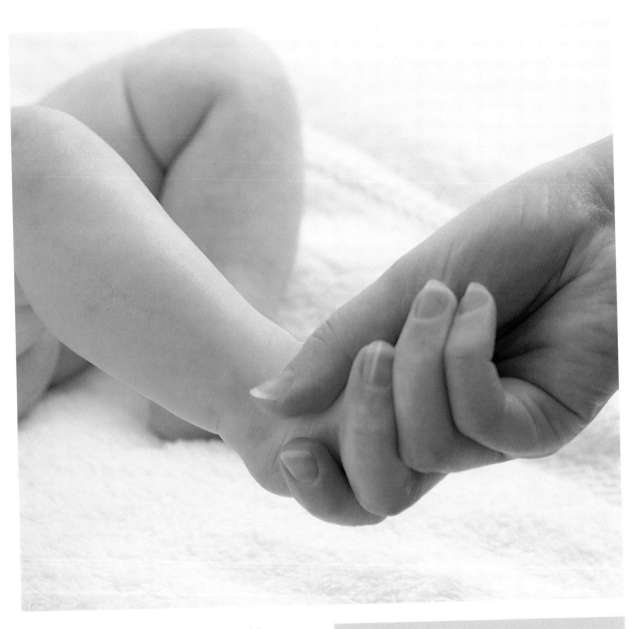

3 Wrapping your whole hand around her ankle, pull the whole foot smoothly through your palms, slightly squeezing the tips of the toes as you pull off the foot.

Repeat the sequence on the other foot.

TIP

During this massage sequence is the ideal time to introduce any reflexology strokes you might feel appropriate.

BACK

The back and spine are the most important part of the framework of the body, both in babies and adults. A strong and flexible back leads to good posture and a balanced body overall. Regular massage will promote all of these, and the use of the back-strengthening routine (see pages 66–7) as your baby develops will help her to sit unaided and, eventually, to stand.

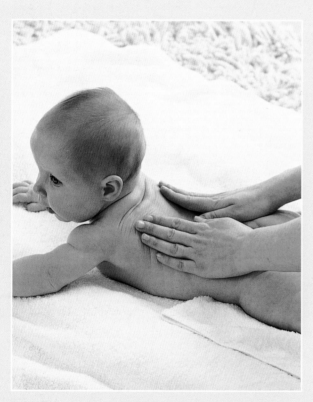

1 Place the flats of your hands on either side of the base of your baby's spine (in small babies you will only be able to use the pads of your fingers) and glide upwards with the effleurage stroke, working across the tops of her shoulders and arms, and down the sides of her torso to the buttocks and backs of her legs, in one long stroke. Repeat this 3–4 times.

2 Using the pads of your thumbs or fingers, massage along either side of her spine in small, circular friction strokes, working upwards from the base of the spine to the top of her shoulders. Repeat this 3–4 times.

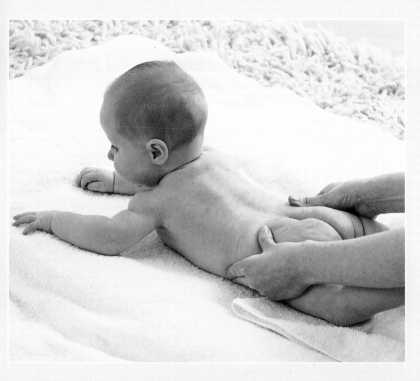

3 Using the same stroke as in step 2, focus on her buttock area, working outwards, along the line of the cheek, from the centre to the outer hip. Massage each side simultaneously. Repeat this 3–4 times.

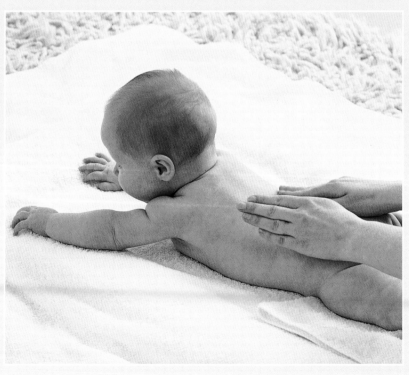

4 Using your cupped hands alternately, gently tap rhythmically all over your baby's back and shoulders and up and down either side of her spine. Do not apply pressure directly to the spine itself. Continue this for 15 seconds.

5 Working horizontally across the back area, place one hand on each side of your baby's torso and, in a wringing action, work up her back from her buttocks to the top of her shoulders. This stroke entails bringing both hands up the sides and over the back to the other side in a synchronized rhythm, pulling up and pushing down. Repeat this 3–4 times.

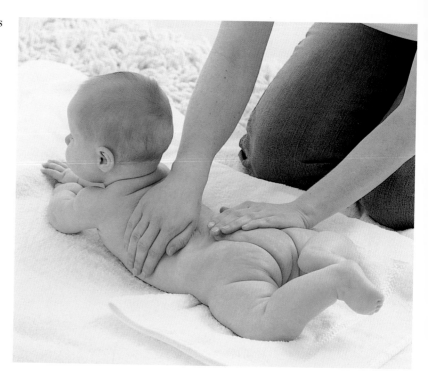

6 Cup one hand around your baby's buttocks and place your other hand on her upper back, gliding it downwards to meet your other hand. Apply gentle pressure to her buttocks before lifting off. Repeat this 3–4 times.

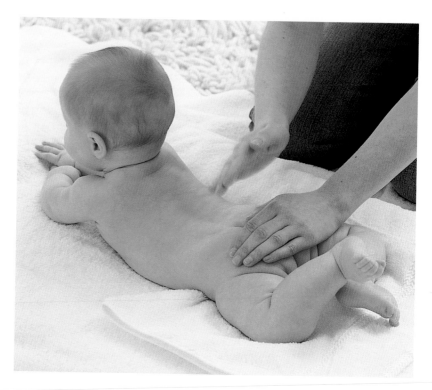

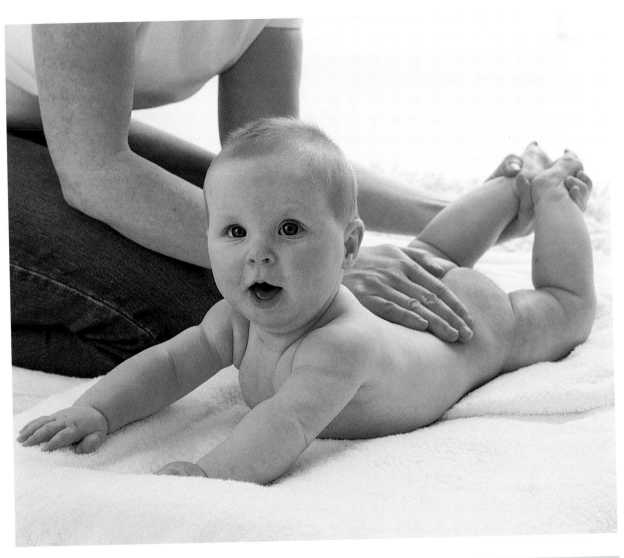

7 Holding your baby's ankles with one hand, lift and stretch her legs very slightly and, with your other hand positioned on her upper back, apply the effleurage stroke along the length of her back and the back of her legs to her feet. Repeat this 3–4 times.

BACK STRENGTHENING

These additional back techniques can be applied to help strengthen the back area once your baby is more developed and can sit aided or unaided. They can be integrated into your normal massage sequence to add variety, or may be used alone as a simple 5-minute routine.

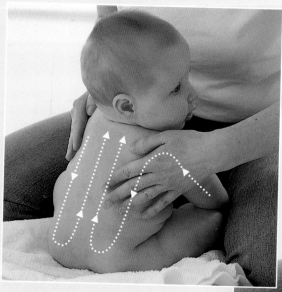

1 With your baby positioned between your legs, leaning in towards you, apply the effleurage stroke with both hands. Glide from the back of her elbows up to the top of her arms, down her back to the base of her spine, and up either side of her spine to the top. This is one long sweeping stroke, pulling up the arms and applying pressure on the downward back stroke before pulling up either side of the spine. Repeat this 3–4 times.

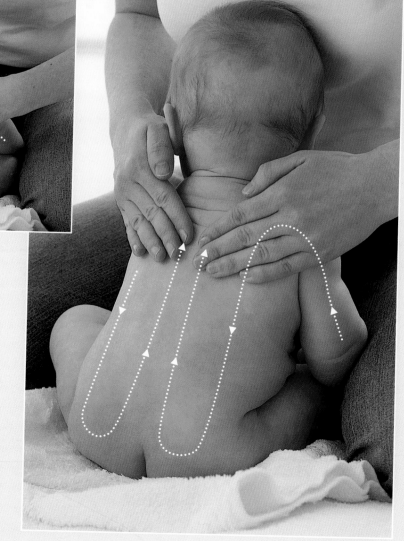

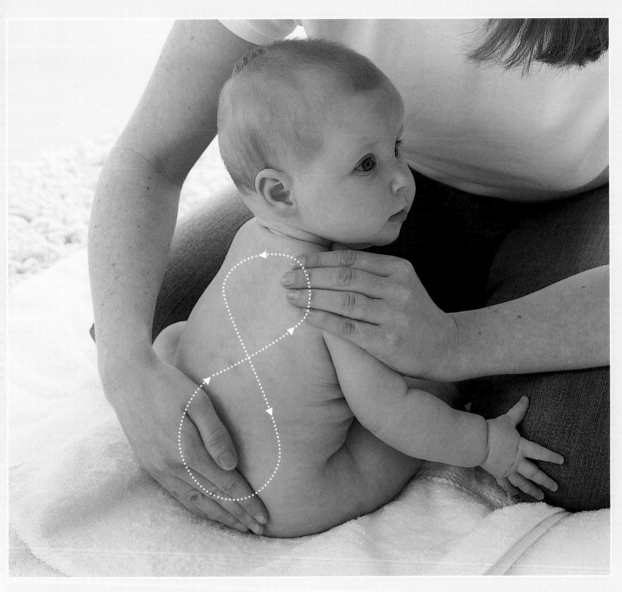

2 In the same position, place one hand on your baby's shoulder to provide support and, with the flat of the other hand, start at the top of the opposite shoulder and make a figure of eight across the whole of her back area. Apply gentle pressure over the tops of her shoulders and the base of her back. Repeat this 3–4 times.

You can also use this sequence with your baby lying down or across your lap. In the sitting position, you can follow on with back, arms and legs if you wish.

FACE

Whether applied to an adult or a baby, facial massage is very calming. At bedtime especially, when your baby is relaxed, it can induce sleep. When massaging the face, remember to take care over sensitive areas, using a minute amount of light oil in order not to drag the skin. It is natural for some babies to resist facial massage until they are more developed.

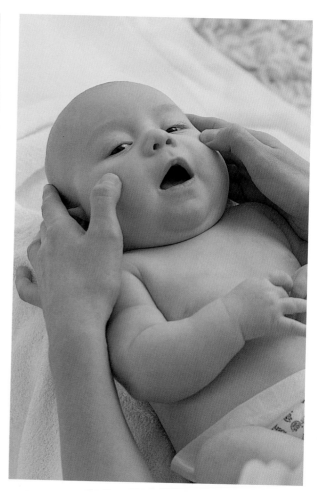

1 With your baby in front of you, cup your hands around his face. Place both thumbs at the centre of his forehead and glide them outwards to the side. Repeat this 3–4 times.

2 Place the pads of your thumbs on either side of your baby's nostrils and glide them outwards, across his cheeks, to the side. Repeat this 3–4 times.

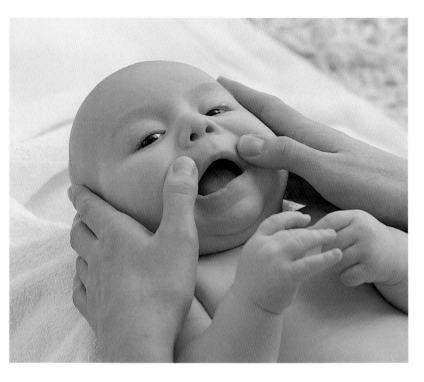

3 Place the pads of your thumbs above your baby's upper lip and glide them outwards and then inwards in a circle around the mouth, finishing at the centre of his chin. Repeat this 3–4 times.

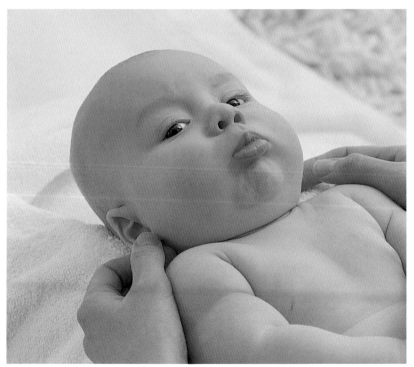

4 Finish the sequence by gently squeezing your baby's ear lobes between your forefingers and thumbs, gently pulling downwards and off.

TIP

As your baby gets older, you may prefer to sit behind him for this massage. In this position, your fingers need to work horizontally across his face in the same sequence.

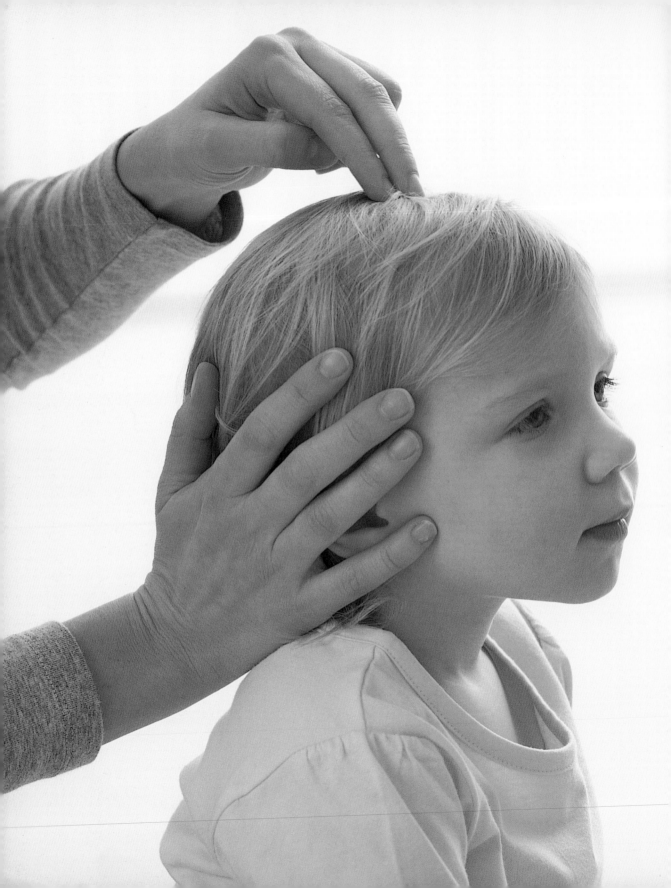

INDIAN HEAD MASSAGE

Indian head massage comes from the ancient medical system of Ayurveda, which has been practised in India for thousands of years. The word Ayurveda is derived from the Sanskrit words ayur, meaning life, and veda, meaning science. Together, ayur and veda combine to form Ayurveda — the science of life. The aim of the ayurvedic system is to treat the person rather than the illness. It also aims to prevent disease and ill health by keeping the body in a constant state of wellbeing.

WHAT IS INDIAN HEAD MASSAGE?

Massage is an important part of Indian life and has been for thousands of years. From the moment babies are born, mothers stroke and rub them in order to help their mobility and general wellbeing, as well as to soothe and calm them. As children grow older, they are taught the art of massage and share the gift with other family members, often learning massage techniques from their grandparents. These rituals help to keep everyone in good health and create a harmonious lifestyle within the home. Mothers massage their babies daily during their first 3 years of life and then reduce this to weekly until the age of 5 or 6 years. After this age, children are independent enough to give and receive massage within the extended family.

Indian head massage is only a small part of the Ayurvedic system but has become very popular around the world, probably because of its feel-good factor and the bonding that occurs between the giver and receiver.

SPECIAL TECHNIQUES

In addition to the massage strokes already described (see pages 20–23), Indian head massage has its own special movements.

Champi

This Hindi word, meaning head massage, is the origin of the word shampoo, which exactly describes the motion of these quick, light and invigorating movements. In true champissage, the sides of the fingers are used in a very gentle rhythmic chopping motion. The hands are placed together, and the stroke is applied by a flick of the wrists working across the area.

Tapping

A form of tapotement (see page 22), this is ideal for stimulating and nourishing the roots of the hair. Less invigorating than *champi*, this quick, rhythmic stroke should feel like raindrops gently falling on the head.

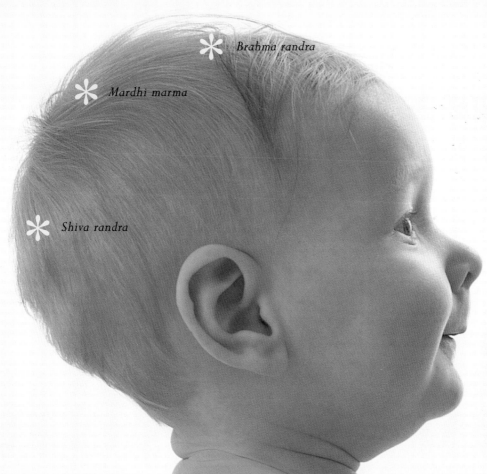

Brahma randra

Mardhi marma

Shiva randra

MARMA POINTS

The word *marma* means secret, or hidden, and vital. The *marma* points are Indian Ayurvedic energy centres, much like Oriental acupressure points. These invisible pathways of energy, or *prana*, connect the physical and the spiritual. Massage or stimulation of these points, sometimes using warm aromatic oils, improves wellbeing. The following three *marma* points are the most important in Indian head massage.

Mardhi marma

This point is situated on the centre of the crown. Place your index fingers above each ear and draw them simultaneously up the scalp until they meet at the top of the head.

Brahma randra

This point is located 3 finger-widths in front of the *mardhi marma* and feels soft in babies.

Shiva randra

This point is found on the back of the head 12 finger-widths from the centre of the hairline. It is situated 4 finger-widths behind the *mardhi marma*.

To stimulate the *marma* points, use the pad of your index finger or thumb to make very small movements in a clockwise direction on the chosen point, spiralling outwards for about 30 circles. Massaging of the *marma* points forms part of the full Indian head massage routine.

The following sequence is particularly suitable for relaxing toddlers and pre-schoolers, and can be incorporated into their night-time routine or used whenever they feel tense or overtired. The whole routine takes only about 10 minutes but, if your child is restless, simply shorten the sequence accordingly. Sit in a position that you both find comfortable.

INDIAN HEAD MASSAGE ROUTINE

1 'Shampoo' your child's head for at least 30 seconds, using the pads of your fingers in brisk, firm movements to stimulate her scalp.

2 Use the pads of your index finger or thumb to stimulate the *marma* points (see page 73). Using small, firm, clockwise movements, spiral in an outwards direction for about 30 circles.

Mardhi marma

Brahma randra

Shiva randra

3 Using your fingertips, gently tap all over your child's scalp, lifting one finger at a time in a pattern like falling raindrops.

4 Place the flats of your hands on the sides of your child's head, with the heel of each hand just above and in front of her ears. Slowly and gently rotate the heel of each hand into the side of her scalp. Repeat this 3–4 times.

5 Squeeze inwards with the heel of each hand, lifting your child's scalp gently. Hold for a few seconds and release. Repeat this twice. Move your hands back into line with the tops of her ears and repeat the stroke.

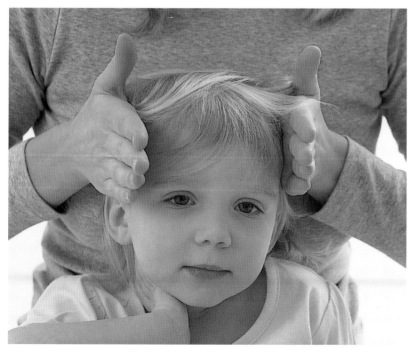

6 Place the palm of each hand in front of your child's ears and over her temples, with your fingers pointing away from you. With the heels of your hands, use slow, wide circular movements to massage the area. Circle 3–4 times.

7 Staying in the same position, draw your hands back on to your child's scalp. Use one hand to support her head and, with the heel of the other hand, gently rub all over the opposite side of her head. Repeat this on the other side.

8 Supporting your child's head with one hand, place the pads of the fingers of your other hand on top of her forehead, along the centre of her hairline. Rotate your fingers firmly, applying pressure downwards on to her scalp. Using a corkscrew motion, work over the top of her head and down into the nape of her neck, returning forwards to the front hairline. Repeat this, covering the midline and the sides of her head.

9 Take strands of your child's hair between the pads of your thumb and index fingers and gently pull the roots of the hair, using each hand alternately in a flow of strokes over her whole head.

10 Champi gently over your child's whole head, using loosely held fingers and wrist action.

11 Rest the backs of your hands on her shoulders, elbows bent and arms relaxed. Apply pressure downwards, then release. Repeat this 3–4 times.

12 Place a hand at the top of each arm and, using a petrissage stroke, knead the arms between your fingers and the heel of your hand, squeezing and pushing upwards. Work gradually down the arm to the elbow and back up.

13 Finish your routine by lovingly stroking your child's head from the front of the hairline to the nape of the neck and then lightly ruffling her entire hair and scalp.

TREATING COMMON AILMENTS

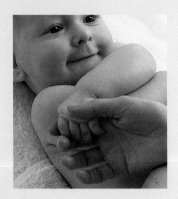

Asthma is a chronic condition of the airways and is commonplace in childhood. Usually, the first signs of the condition in a baby or toddler are shallow or laboured breathing followed by coughing or wheezing. Children living in a city environment are often more prone to asthma because of pollution. The majority of children 'grow out' of childhood asthma and their breathing reverts to normal.

ASTHMA – MASSAGE

Massage is a helpful way of relieving the symptoms of asthma, but should not be applied during an acute attack. However, it can help to reduce the anxiety caused in the sub-acute stage. Do not insist on massaging your baby or toddler if he appears uncomfortable with your touch. This routine is aimed at opening up the chest and can be done through clothing.

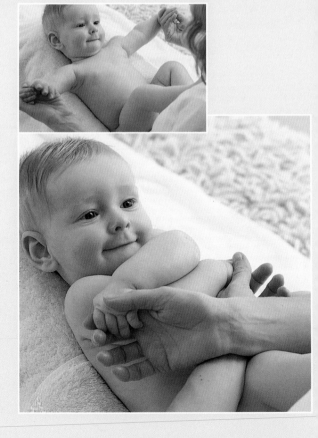

1 Position your baby or toddler along your thighs, so that he is facing you, then take his legs and place them at either side of your waist for security. Holding his arms at the wrist, open them out to the sides simultaneously in a gentle stretch and then bring them back, crossed over his chest, first one way and then the other. Make this stretching exercise part of play. Repeat this 3–4 times.

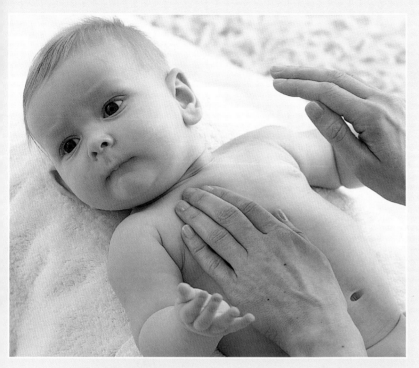

2 Place your hands on either side of your baby's breastbone and, with a cupping action, gently apply pressure with alternate hands in a rhythmic flow. Work your way all over the centre and sides of his chest. Repeat this for about 30 seconds.

3 Turn your baby over so that he is lying on his stomach, still positioned on your thighs. Still using the cupping action, apply gentle pressure all over his back and sides. This is a percussion stroke and, applied in this position, may cause your baby to vomit slightly. This is no cause for concern: it is due to the cupping action compressing the bronchial tubes and helping to expel any excess mucus, which in turn will help breathing.

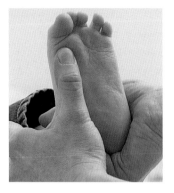

In cases of minor asthmatic attacks, apply either the pressure point or the circling technique to stimulate the main respiratory points. This helps to relax the tension in the bronchial tubes, calm spasmodic breathing and reduce coughing. Applying pressure to the solar plexus reflex point will encourage the release of anxiety and panic, which can exacerbate the symptoms of a sudden attack.

ASTHMA - REFLEXOLOGY

1 SOLAR PLEXUS: Place your thumbs over the solar plexus reflex point of each foot. Allow your child to press against your thumbs. Repeat this 2–3 times.

2 TRACHEA: Working on your child's right foot, press or circle over the trachea reflex point. This is the padded area just below the big toe. Repeat this 2–3 times.

3 LUNGS: Caterpillar-walk, press and circle over the lung reflex point, which is the padded area below toes 2–5, on your child's right foot. Repeat this 2–3 times.

Repeat steps 2–3 on the left foot.

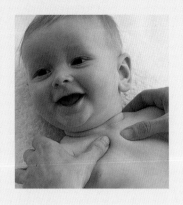

In the early months, babies breathe through their mouth, so build-up of mucus (known as catarrh) may be manageable during the day. However, it can be very uncomfortable at night, leading to broken sleep. Placing your baby in a more upright sleeping position will help to provide relief at night. You can do this by raising one end of the cot or, more easily, by placing extra padding beneath the mattress.

CATARRH – MASSAGE

Massage is very effective in helping to loosen phlegm. If it is used alongside conventional medical treatment, it can help to expel any build-up of mucus from a baby's airways. The most comfortable position for this massage is to place your baby on your raised knees so that he is facing you and in a position that makes breathing comfortable.

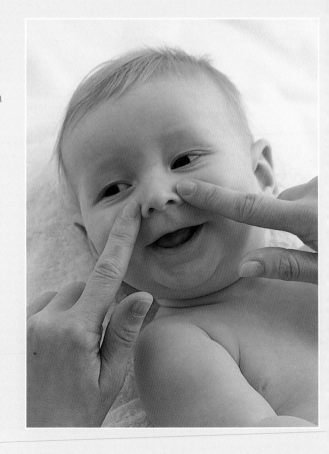

1 Place the pads of your index fingers on either side of your baby's nostrils. Apply gentle pressure and release without losing contact. Repeat this 3–4 times.

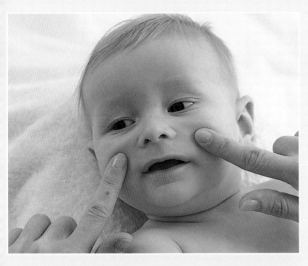

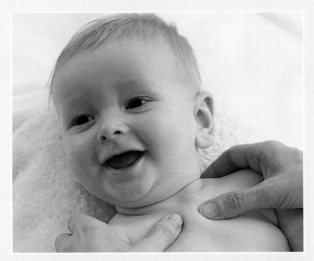

2 Following the natural curve of your baby's face, move your index fingers simultaneously downwards and outwards along the sinuses, using the underside of his cheekbones as a guide. Lift off and return to the starting position. Repeat this 3–4 times.

3 Move down to your baby's chest and place the thumb pads on either side of his breastbone. Making very small circles, work across the top of his chest, outwards to the top of his arms. Repeat this 3–4 times.

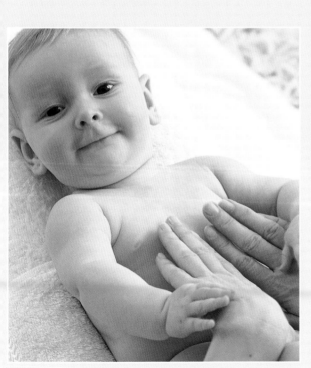

4 Using the flat of your hands in an effleurage stroke, apply gentle pressure and work from the centre of his chest outwards and return to the centre. Repeat the stroke slightly lower than before and work your way down the whole of his chest in a continuous flow, each stroke slightly overlapping the previous one. Repeat this 3–4 times.

TIP

These movements help to relieve congestion by relaxing your baby's chest muscles, thus making breathing easier. With an older baby, it is safe to apply professionally mixed essential oils, such as eucalyptus and lavender, to relieve catarrh.

Stimulating the following reflex points will help to relieve the nasal discomfort and congestion often caused by teething, colds and viruses. Confidently applying the pressure and circling techniques will relieve the pain caused by the pressure of mucus build-up, encourage the removal of mucus waste and promote easy breathing. Stimulating the head reflex point will also encourage relaxation and sleep.

CATARRH - REFLEXOLOGY

1 HEAD: Working on the right foot, press and circle over the head reflex point, which is the padded area of the big toe. Repeat this 2–3 times.

2 SINUSES: Press, circle and glide your thumb up along the backs of toes 2–5 to stimulate the sinus reflex. Repeat this twice.

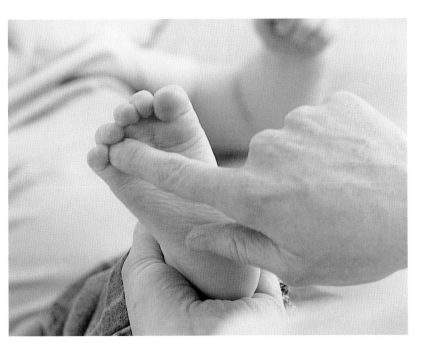

3 EARS: Press into the ear reflex point, which lies at the base of toes 4 and 5, above the lung reflex point. Repeat this 2–3 times.

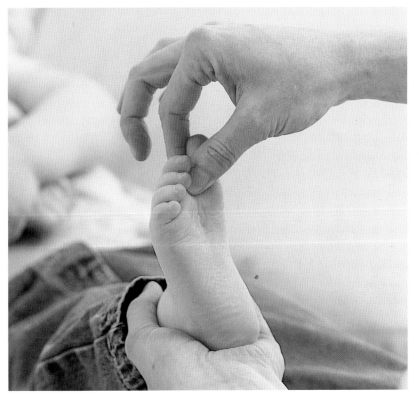

4 LYMPHATICS: Press down gently between each toe with your thumb and index finger to stimulate the lymphatic reflex point of the head and chest. This will help to boost your child's immune system and assist the release of toxins. Repeat this twice.

Repeat steps 1–4 on the left foot.

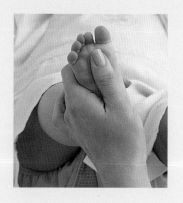

Restless sleep or the inability to settle is not uncommon in young babies and can have a variety of causes. If you are satisfied that your baby is not unwell, but just restless due to teething or overtiredness, for example, then the soothing effects of reflexology on her nervous system can be of great benefit. Follow the steps below to induce a state of relaxation. Your baby will soon feel calm and ready for sleep.

SLEEP – REFLEXOLOGY

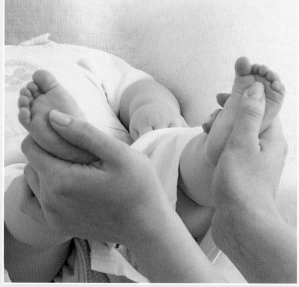

1 HEAD: Working on your baby's right foot, press and circle over the head reflex point, which is the padded area of the big toe. Repeat this 2–3 times.

2 SOLAR PLEXUS: Place your thumbs over the solar plexus reflex point of each foot. Allow your baby to press against your thumbs. Repeat this 2–3 times.

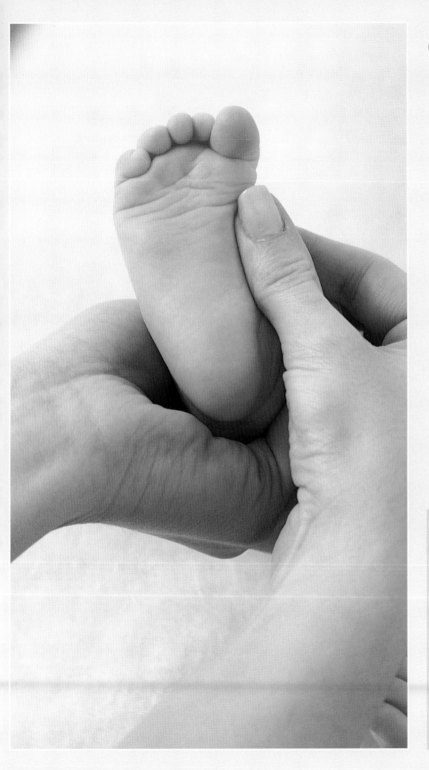

3 SPINE: Caterpillar-walk or glide your thumb from your baby's inner heel to the top of her big toe. Repeat this 2–3 times.

Repeat steps 1 and 3 on the left foot.

TIP

The ideal time to perform these simple steps is directly after your baby's evening bath when she is warm, cosy and clean. Don't forget to complement this soothing treatment with an environment of blissful, soft lighting and a gentle, encouraging voice.

Digestive complaints such as colic and constipation respond very well to massage and stretching. However, it may be some time before you see any significant improvement so you should persevere and apply the techniques for several weeks. The ideal time to massage for these conditions is during a nappy change, when your baby will already be in a face-up position on the floor or changing mat.

DIGESTIVE COMPLAINTS - MASSAGE

Colic is common in babies up to the age of 3 months. Theories about its causes range from feeding problems, dietary intolerance, environment or immaturity of the digestive system. However, it lasts for a very short time and is a distressing pattern of crying, not an illness.

Constipation, the infrequent and painful passage of hard stools, is more common in bottle-fed babies, who may have 2 or 3 bowel movements a day, than in breast-fed babies, who absorb most of the breast milk, so that there is little residue to pass. In order to prevent constipation, ensure that your baby is getting enough fluids in his diet — and fibre if he is on solids.

RECOGNIZING COLIC
If you answer 'yes' to the following questions, your baby is probably suffering from colic.
* Is he under 3 months old?
* Does he cry more at certain times of day, particularly in the early evening?
* Does his stomach feel 'hard' and does it rumble?
* Does he draw up his legs as if in pain?
* Is his crying high-pitched and distressed, especially after feeding?

HOW YOU CAN HELP
* Position your baby correctly during and after feeding to reduce the build-up of uncomfortable pockets of gas in his digestive system.
* If you are breast-feeding, avoid eating gas-producing foods, dairy foods, chocolate and caffeine
* If you are bottle-feeding, try giving your baby smaller but more frequent amounts, supplemented with bottled water.

MASSAGING THE ABDOMEN

To relax your baby's abdomen before massage, try a few playful feathering strokes over the area before placing the flat of your hand in a holding position ready to commence.

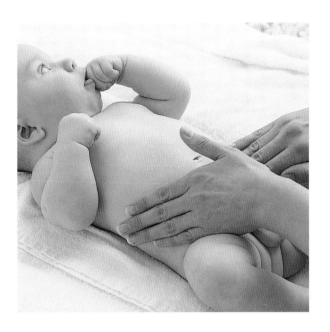

1 With the flat of your hands, and using even, relaxed effleurage strokes, work down the right side of the abdomen, between the lower rib, hip and navel, hand over hand. Continue for 2–3 minutes and then repeat on the left side. It is important to work first right and then left in order to follow the natural flow of the contents of the colon.

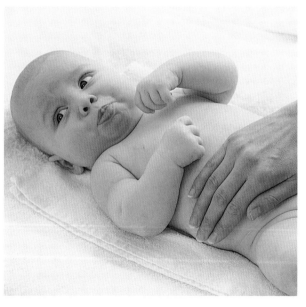

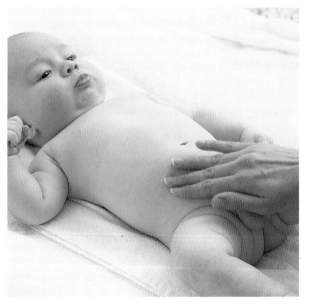

2 Place your hand horizontally, squeeze very gently and knead from side to side using cupped effleurage. There should be no downward pressure, the idea being to work across the stomach in order to promote relaxation. Spend about 30 seconds on this.

3 With your hand still cupped, massage the abdomen using a circular motion, working clockwise, from left to right. Repeat this 3–4 times.

4 With the pads of your fingers, make small gentle circles with even pressure around the navel area in a clockwise direction. Be careful not to cause discomfort over the bladder. Repeat this 3–4 times.

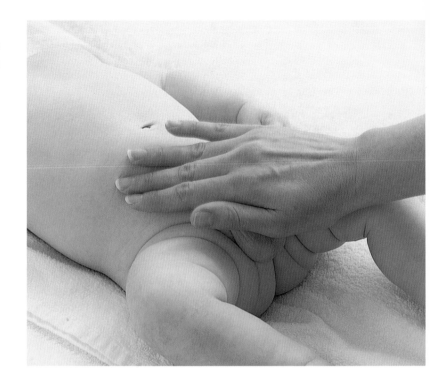

5 Continue using the pads of your fingers, this time working on the solar plexus. This is the area beneath the ribcage, at the centre of the upper abdomen. Make very small circles in a clockwise direction, as before, and use even pressure. Repeat this 3–4 times.

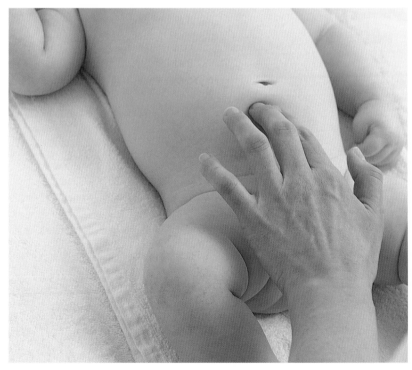

LEG STRETCHES

Leg stretches are very effective but it's important to make sure that they are only undertaken when your baby's muscles are warm and relaxed. Applying them after a massage routine is ideal. Babies often enjoy this gentle movement, which can be made into play. If your baby shows any resistance to the stretches, use a very gentle shaking movement to encourage him to relax.

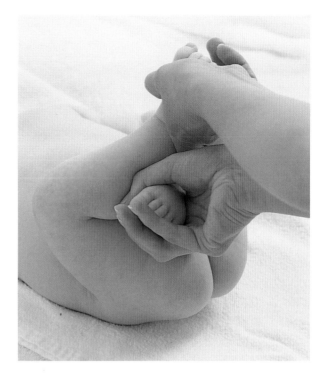

1 Continuing with your baby in the lying position, take his ankles in either hand and cross them over while, at the same time, bringing them towards the abdomen. Then stretch them out straight, pulling them gently towards you.

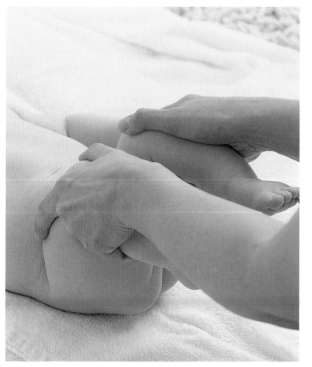

2 Pull his knees together up towards his abdomen and then stretch them out straight. Repeat, this time rotating them each way, and finish by stretching them out straight.

TIP

An alternative to leg stretches is the 'colic dance': gently swaying your baby backwards and forwards and then up and down, bending his knees. Do this with your baby held slightly away from you so that you can remain in eye contact during the 'dance'.

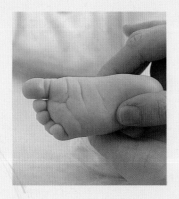

Stimulating the reflex points of the digestive system on your baby's feet can help a range of abdominal complaints, from constipation to colic. Reflexology will stimulate a sluggish bowel, aid removal of bodily waste, regulate bowel movements and ease abdominal discomfort. It can also help to relieve the pain of abdominal spasms, a symptom often associated with colic in babies.

DIGESTIVE COMPLAINTS – REFLEXOLOGY

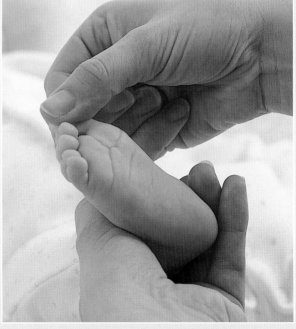

1 SOLAR PLEXUS: Place your thumbs over the solar plexus reflex point of each foot. Allow your baby to press against your thumbs. Repeat this 2–3 times.

2 HEAD: Working on the right foot, press and circle over the head reflex point, which is the padded area of the big toe. Repeat this 2–3 times.

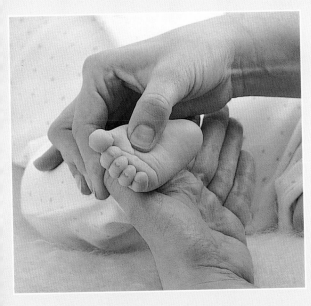

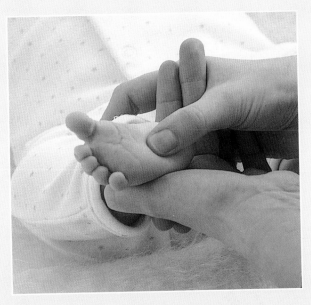

3 STOMACH: Working on your baby's right foot, press and circle over the stomach reflex point. This is just below the trachea reflex point. Repeat this 2–3 times.

4 SMALL INTESTINE: Caterpillar-walk, press and circle over the small intestine reflex point. This lies above the padded area of your baby's heel. Repeat this 2–3 times.

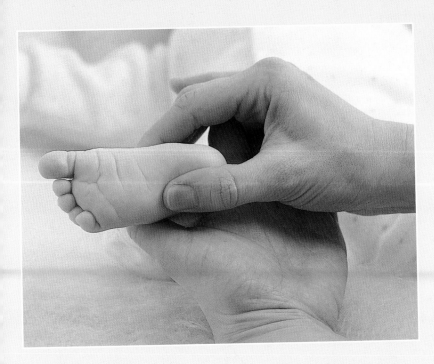

5 COLON: Caterpillar-walk or glide your thumb through the entire colon reflex point from right foot to left continuously over your baby's heels (see page 29). Repeat this 2–3 times.

Repeat steps 2–4 on the left foot.

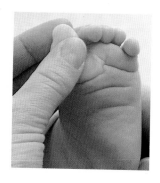

Skin problems can range from cradle cap to eczema or psoriasis and are seldom caused by external factors in young babies. Some skin conditions are associated with food allergies, so it may be advisable to look at your baby's diet. Stimulation of the following reflex points will calm and rebalance your baby's hormone system. This will help relieve stress, which is also associated with skin complaints.

SKIN PROBLEMS – REFLEXOLOGY

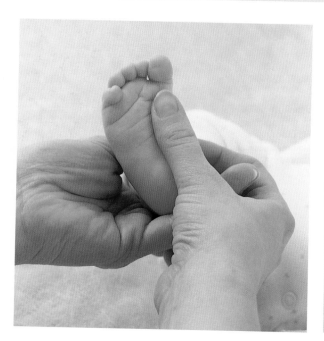

1 ZONE-WALKING: Starting on the right foot, caterpillar-walk or glide your thumb through each zone. Start with zone 1, which runs from the heel to the big toe. Repeat this sequence twice.

2 SOLAR PLEXUS: Place your thumbs over the solar plexus reflex point of each foot. Allow your baby to press against your thumbs. Repeat this 2–3 times.

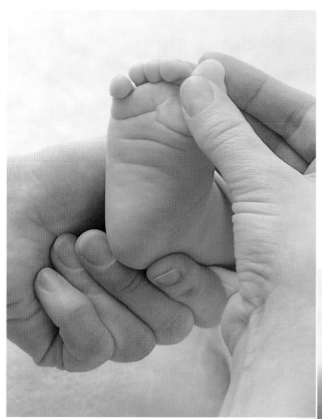

3 TOE PRESSURE: With your thumb, gently press then circle over the pad of each toe, working from the big toe to the little toe of the right foot. Repeat this twice.

Repeat steps 1 and 3 on the left foot.

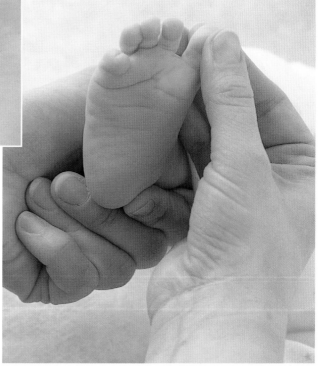

A baby's first tooth usually appears between the sixth and eighth month. However, babies may show signs of teething long before any teeth appear. They often seem irritable and distressed because of the pain and discomfort caused by the teeth erupting through the gums. Another side-effect of teething is the production of excess saliva which, when swallowed, may cause slight looseness of the bowels.

TEETHING – MASSAGE

Gently massaging your baby's cheeks along the gum line may relieve some of the discomfort of teething, but most babies prefer to receive soothing strokes to the body, which lift their mood by stimulating the 'happy' endorphins. Homeopathic remedies, such as teething granules, may help if symptoms persist.

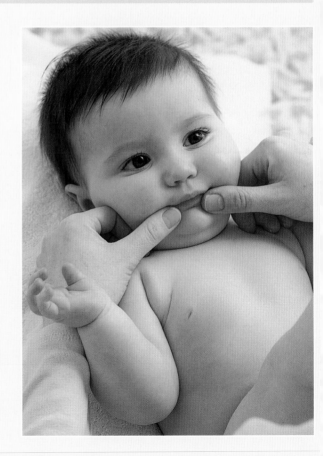

1 With your baby positioned on your lap or thighs, place the pads of your thumbs above his upper lip and apply gentle massage in a circle along the gum line outwards towards his cheeks and then inwards around the bottom of the mouth, finishing at the centre of his chin. Repeat this 3–4 times.

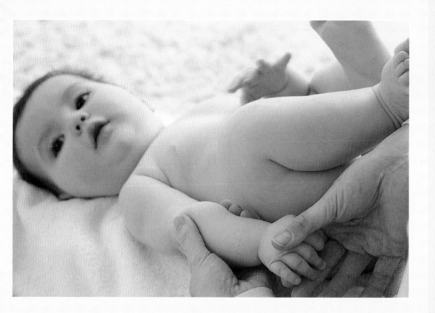

2 Take one hand between your thumb and fingers and gently squeeze and stroke it, working from the wrist to the tips of the fingers. Repeat on the other hand.

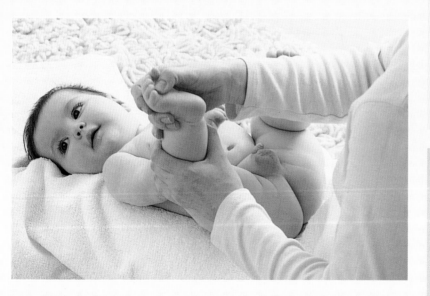

3 Move down to the feet. With your thumb and fingers stroke and squeeze the tops and soles of one foot. Use a gentle but firm touch so as not to create a tickling sensation. Repeat on the other foot.

THE DEVELOPMENT OF TEETH

The development of the teeth varies enormously and it is not unknown for babies to be born with teeth. However, in general, the first teeth to appear are the two front incisors, at about 6–8 months of age, followed by the lateral incisors at about 9 months of age. The cheek teeth (pre-molars) appear between 10 and 14 months of age and the canines (fangs) at 16–18 months. A child will not have a full set of baby teeth (milk teeth) until he is 24–30 months old. These will be replaced by permanent teeth by about the age of 6 years, while the wisdom teeth do not appear until at least the late teens, giving a full set of 32 permanent teeth.

TIP

To end your massage, you may choose to cuddle your baby to you and, with long strokes, gently work up and down the length of his back, covering the whole area. This is very comforting and non-intrusive, and you can accompany it with soft talking or singing.

Teething can make your baby feel very miserable, affecting both her sleep and her mood. Help to relieve these symptoms by applying the simple pressure, circling and gliding techniques to the teeth and sinus reflex points. This will ease discomfort and help to pacify your baby. Stimulating the lymphatic system reflex points will also encourage a healthy immune system and ward off infection.

TEETHING - REFLEXOLOGY

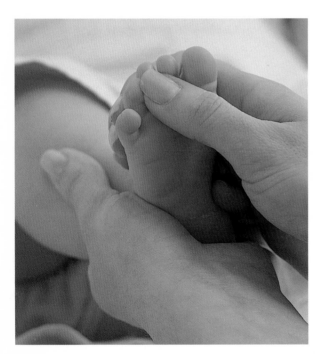

1 SINUSES: Starting with the right foot, press, circle and glide your thumb up along the backs of toes 2–5 to stimulate the sinus reflex. Repeat this 2–3 times.

2 TEETH: Caterpillar-walk or press on the teeth reflex points. These are on the front of each toe, from the nail to the base of the toe joint. Repeat this 2–3 times.

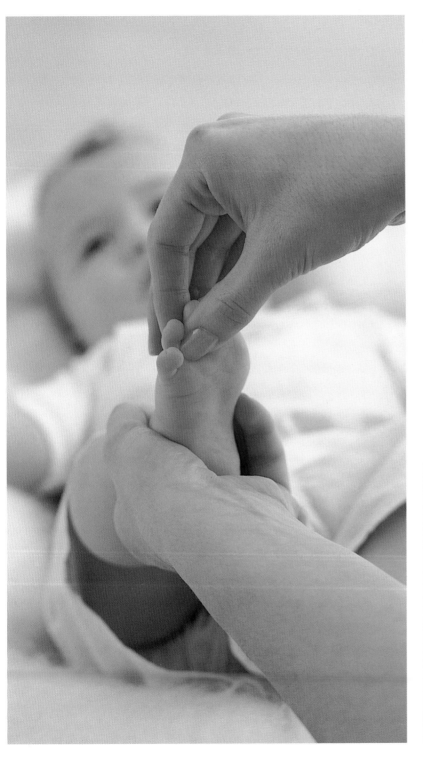

3 LYMPHATICS: Press down gently between each toe with your thumb and finger to stimulate the lymphatic region of the head and chest. This will help to boost her immune system and assist the release of toxins. Repeat this twice.

Repeat steps 1–3 on the left foot.

TIP

An irritable baby can lead to a tired and irritable mother or father. Reflexology can be of great benefit to you both, allowing you the gift of quality time spent with your child, which is not only soothing and relaxing, but is also an expression of your love and tenderness.

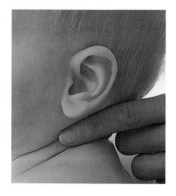

Always consult a doctor if your baby is showing symptoms of earache, as this may indicate an ear infection. There are also simple techniques to relieve earache that can be used alongside conventional treatment and to prevent conditions such as 'glue ear'. You can include this sequence in the full massage routine or use it alone and finish by squeezing both your baby's ear lobes between your thumbs and forefingers.

EARACHE – MASSAGE

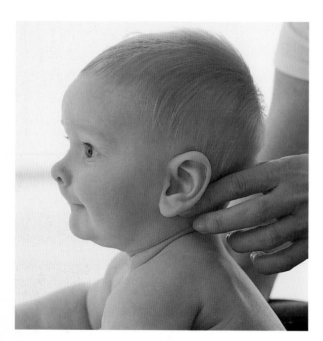

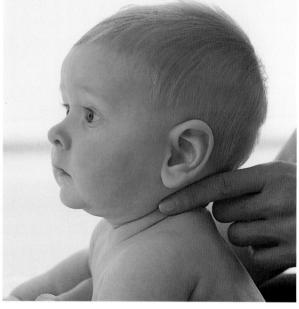

1 With your baby in front of you, facing forwards, place the pad of your index finger behind the earlobe, on the side of his head. Apply light pressure while supporting his head with your free hand.

2 Find the natural hollow at the top of your baby's upper jawbone, press gently and then move downwards, following the edge of the jawbone towards the throat. Keep the movement smooth, applying even pressure.

GLUE EAR

Glue ear is a sticky, glue-like discharge from the middle ear, hence the name. It prevents the eardrum from working normally and can result in partial deafness. Therefore, if your baby or toddler has any discharge other than regular earwax, you should consult your doctor immediately. Cranial osteopathy, which involves manipulation of the bones of the skull with a light, non-invasive touch, can help cases of glue ear.

3 Return your finger to the starting position. Now draw it downwards at an angle towards you, following the base of the skull.

Repeat these steps 3–4 times, then repeat on the other side of the head. The steps may also be performed simultaneously on both sides of your baby's head.

TIP

Regular use of this technique helps to prevent build-up of wax or discharge. Incorporate it into your baby's hair-washing routine for convenience.

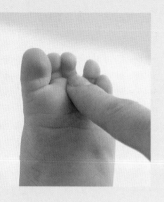

The following reflex points can help to relieve mild earache when stimulated and boost your baby's immune system to help fight infection. Earache is often associated with sinus congestion and so you may wish to include the sinus reflex points on page 27 for an effective all-round treatment. Consult your doctor if you suspect that your child is suffering from an infection of the middle ear.

EARACHE – REFLEXOLOGY

1 HEAD: Working on the right foot, press and circle over the head reflex point, which is the padded area of the big toe. Repeat this 2–3 times.

2 EARS: Press into the ear reflex point, which lies at the base of toes 4 and 5, above the lung reflex point. Repeat this 2–3 times.

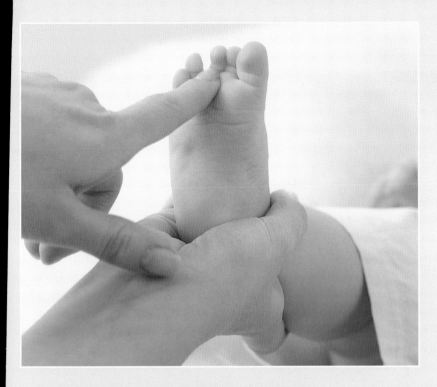

3 EUSTACHIAN TUBES: Press down with your thumb or finger into the Eustachian tube reflex point, which lies between toes 3 and 4. Repeat this 2–3 times.

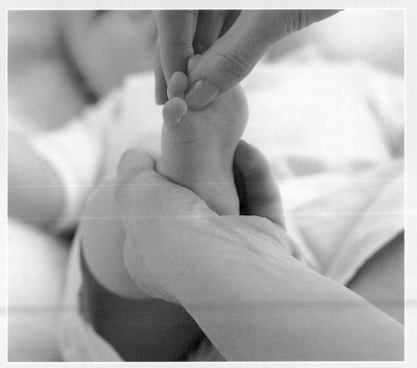

4 LYMPHATICS: Press down gently between each toe with your thumb and index finger to stimulate the lymphatic region of the head and chest. This will help to boost your child's immune system and assist the release of toxins. Repeat this twice.

Repeat steps 1–4 on the left foot.

INDEX

ACKNOWLEDGEMENTS

I would like to thank all my dear family and friends who
have let me 'share' their babies over the years.
Wendy Kavanagh

Executive Editor Jane McIntosh
Project Editor Leanne Bryan
Executive Art Editor Leigh Jones
Design Miranda Harvey
Senior Production Controller Martin Croshaw
Picture Researcher Sophie Delpech

**Special Photography © Octopus Publishing Group
Limited**/Russell Sadur.
**Other photography Octopus Publishing Group
Limited**/Mike Prior 4;/Ian Wallace 25 bottom.